GW00374699

10 Steps to Innovation Heaven

10 Steps to Innovation Heaven

How to create future growth and competitive strength

Howard Wright

CYAN

Marshall Cavendish
Business

Copyright © 2007 Howard Wright

First published in 2007 by:

Marshall Cavendish Limited
119 Wardour Street
London W1F 0UW
United Kingdom
T: +44 (0)20 7565 6000
F: +44 (0)20 7734 6221
E: sales@marshallcavendish.co.uk
Online bookstore: www.marshallcavendish.co.uk

and

Cyan Communications Limited
119 Wardour Street
London W1F 0UW
United Kingdom
T: +44 (0)20 7565 6120
E: sales@cyanbooks.com
www.cyanbooks.com

The right of Howard Wright to be identified as the author of this work has been asserted by him in accordance with the Copyright, Designs and Patents Act 1988.

All rights reserved

No part of this publication may be reproduced, stored in a retrieval system or transmitted in any form or by any means including photocopying, electronic, mechanical, recording or otherwise, without the prior written permission of the rights holders, application for which must be made to the publisher.

A CIP record for this book is available from the British Library

ISBN-13 978-1-905736-05-8
ISBN-10 1-905736-05-3

Designed and typeset by Curran Publishing Services, Norwich, UK

Printed and bound in Great Britain by
TJ International Ltd, Padstow, Cornwall

Contents

Appendices

Figures

Preface

This is a book of two halves. First, as the title suggests, it introduces the steps that will help individuals and organisations bring Innovation into their daily lives and initiatives. Not just for the short term, but by making Innovation 'sticky', creating a culture of change within a company. The book is also a personal journey of discovery – a distillation of some of the key learning points and lessons as well as the ups and downs of being 'slightly' different. When these two flow together the journey becomes alive and, I hope, of interest to a wide audience – those interested in Innovation itself and also those interested in self-discovery.

Howard Wright
www.stickyinnovation.com

Chapter 1
Introduction

Innovation has become a byword for the new, interesting and exciting things in our lives. The word appears in a large number of magazine articles, advertisements and the media in general all around the world. A Google search in August 2006 for the word Innovation resulted in over 78 million web pages; a similar search in August 2005 had produced only 43 million, so it seems our obsession with the concept continues to grow.

In the business world too, the word Innovation is thrown around in boardrooms, team meetings and marketing groups. It has become synonymous with change, strategy, marketing and any other 'new' activity businesses undertake. A search in 2006 through reports and accounts in the USA and UK revealed that over 65 per cent of them contained the word Innovation in one context or another.

Although it is often talked about, however, few people have a real idea about what it truly is and, more importantly, how you can actually do something about it. Innovation has become the answer to many companies' problems and is seen as the Holy Grail – 'If only we could be more innovative we would succeed.' Many companies try to get 'some of this Innovation' and set up teams or initiatives without really understanding what they are trying to achieve, or more importantly how they would know if they had some! And of course those that adopt this approach are always disappointed as they never achieve what they set out to – whatever that was.

This book is a documentation of an Innovation journey, my journey, over a 12-year period working in the field of Innovation. It is written from both a business and a personal perspective. The start of this journey, like so many things in my life, was accidental. In 1994 the company I worked for had set up a working party to look at selling off one of its business units. As I had a technology background and was head of a large telecommunications team for the company, I was brought in to look at the technological impacts of the sale. It soon became apparent to me that the impact on the company was not going to come from the sale but from technology and the Internet, and the impact these two things would have on the wider organisation. I persuaded the team to allow me to put together an appendix explaining my thoughts, and this was included in the report to the board. The appendix ended up becoming the report and the report the appendix. My journey into the world of strategy, foresight, creative thinking and Innovation had begun – a journey that would change my life for ever and one that would take me into new and exciting areas I could only have dreamed of.

The response to the report was to set up an Innovation team – the first I had ever heard of and a bold move for a large monopoly company. It was apparent that it was facing the threat of unprecedented change in its market, and like many organisations it was unclear what to do about it. The first signs of the Internet were emerging from the USA; technology and more interestingly email were starting to have an effect on the way people communicated, albeit at this time only on proprietary systems.

Trying to explain these discontinuities to the 'non-believers' in the organisation became my mission, my passion. To many I seemed to be talking a different language – I think they thought I was from a different planet. However my belief was so strong that I persisted and as the activity didn't 'fit' into any ordinary organisational model the Innovation and Futures team was formed and as they say the 'rest is history'.

Ever since this first foray into Innovation I have been part of, or leading, an Innovation team and have experienced Innovation from the sharp end. I have worked with many hundreds of companies all over the world on Innovation initiatives, built new environments, and developed new tools and techniques. In this book I have documented my experiences, the things that I have learned, the insights I have gained and the experiences, both positive and negative, I have had. This book will provide readers with tools and techniques that can be employed not only at work but in their personal lives. The book outlines a 10-step approach to Innovation – a framework for making things happen, taking ideas into action.

Like many working in the field in those early days, I thought Innovation was just about having bright ideas. I assumed it was synonymous with creativity – the new and exciting things in life. However I learned the hard way that just having great ideas is not enough to make a real difference. Although that is a key part of any Innovation activity, the real secret is to give these great ideas some persistence, to make something happen and create true Innovation that sticks!

Although this book is targeted towards making Innovation a reality within a commercial environment, the lessons learned and the tools and techniques discussed are applicable to a wide range of personal and business situations.

But why is Innovation important?

Innovation has for many years been seen as vital to the success of businesses around the world, particularly those faced with market change. Although much has been written about the subject, most of it has been theoretical and based on interpreted case studies, not practical no-nonsense guidance and advice on how to really do it – making Innovation a reality.

Globalisation, and lower-cost manufacturing and labour, coupled with cheap and effective mass communication are changing the business world around us. The changes are massive and very often discontinuous and unpredictable. The unstable nature of this new commercial environment is forcing companies all over the world to react and become more flexible in their approach to change.

Governments around the world have also recognised the need to do things differently and have put in place large programmes to try and engender new approaches and develop new ways of working, hoping to provide some unique selling point for their particular region or country. Similarly, local government agencies and non-governmental organisations are also trying to encourage Innovation and change. However all this focus and activity is less than effective as none of them actually define what they mean by Innovation; if you look at their prospectuses and manifestos, Innovation means whatever they want it to – from better law and order to cleaner streets and new businesses, and the list goes on and on!

The traditionally slow change in business models in the 1980s and 1990s has accelerated dramatically, with new ways of doing business being 'invented' almost on a daily basis. Your great idea or new business concept can become a reality in less time than it took historically to write a business plan and find the finance. The fast-moving and open nature of this new commercial environment allows anybody with an idea to become an entrepreneur – quickly and at very low cost.

In 2001 I was in San Francisco for a conference, and on the way back from the conference centre I got talking to a woman on a trolley-bus – not something I would normally do! She told me she was in town to celebrate a business deal: she had just become a millionaire by selling her company to a large US retail chain. The idea behind her company was simple: she had set up a website that allowed diabetics to enter their blood sugar level and would then print out a menu for the day which would provide the necessary sugar and other nutrients to rebalance their system. The idea came to her when her sister was diagnosed as diabetic; she was an avid cook and thought that diet could be used to help rebalance sugar levels. She started by developing recipes for her sister and then whole menus. The idea seemed to be something that worked. It had taken her less than six months to take the idea from a concept to a million-dollar business. This to me was a classic example of Innovation in action: she had built a connection between two seemingly disparate parts of her life and created a whole new business idea. Traditionally this idea would probably never got off the ground. How would a woman from a small farming community find the sponsor, the finance and the advice on how to turn her idea into a reality? The Internet and a nephew enabled her to build a website. The website evolved quickly and within less than three weeks had gained a global audience and the attention of some large players. It provided her with a way of realising her idea in just the way she wanted, in a cost-effective manner with a secure payment channel, all for less than $5000.

> Never has the gap between what you believe and what you can achieve been so small – if you can dream it you can do it.

This example is one of probably millions of business models that are emerging from the new world we live in. The first response of many larger, established companies to this fast-moving, rapidly evolving environment is to attempt to reduce bottom-line costs, taking people and fixed costs out of the equation as quickly as possible. I liken this approach to them becoming the most efficient dinosaurs on the planet. Meanwhile the mammals, their competition, are evolving all around and will soon dominate the world, while the dinosaurs slowly wither and die or are hit by a cataclysmic change.

Although this drive to efficiency is a viable short-term tactical response it cannot be a long-term viable strategy for survival. Top-line growth through Innovation and Innovative activities, has got to be on the corporate and individual agenda if companies are going to maintain a viable position in the new global economic balance. 'Companies cannot grow through cost reduction and reengineering alone. ... Innovation is the key element in providing aggressive top-line growth, and for increasing bottom-line results' (Tony Davila, Mark J. Epstein and Robert Shelton, *Making innovation work*).

So why this 10-step approach?

The idea for the general approach to Innovation came to me late in 2000 when I was at Boston Logan airport waiting for a flight back home to the UK after visiting MIT. I had been at a very tedious conference on some obscure topic and had come up with a great idea for a new service that my company could offer and, in my opinion, become market leader in a new area. The challenge was how to get the company to take it up – how to make it listen to what I had to say and benefit from the huge revenue stream that could be created. Being a 'creative type' I had these ideas on a frequent basis, but nothing ever came of them because I couldn't make my voice heard. I was seen as something of an oddity, and although people were usually interested in talking to me I guess I was not usually taken seriously.

As I usually do, being a good 'innovative person', I purchased a bunch of magazines on a wide range of topics to read as I waited for the flight. I have always been a curious person, so the more obscure the magazine the better – they give stimulus and new perspectives on your world. (My local postal delivery person must really be fed up with the number of magazines I get delivered. I once counted I 'consumed' over 25 magazines per month on average!)

One of the articles was on the subject of bees and posed the question 'Why do bees swarm?' The accepted theory had been that the queen bee became restless and decided that it was time to move on to a new location. However, further study had showed that in fact it is the outside of the hive that gets restless – perhaps finding a new food source – and moves en masse; interestingly the queen then has to follow. This concept fascinated me and I got to thinking about the organisation as a beehive and wondering whether there was a parallel in organisations – building a link between my problem of getting my idea heard and the bees.

If an organisation was viewed as a hive and the CEO/Board was the queen, how could I stir the outside of the hive to move and get it interested in a new food source – in this case my idea? If the model was valid, disturbing the outside of the hive could change the organisation, and the senior management and the company would have to follow. An interesting if challenging concept.

I had seen so many instances of top-down led change failing because the leaders couldn't make the change stick. There was something about the 'thou shalt' characteristics of the top-down approach that seemed to be stopping change being effective, so the idea of changing the organisation from the outside in seemed to be one that might work. Anyway it was worth a try!

> First they ignore you, then they laugh at you, then they fight you, then you win.
>
> Mahatma Gandhi

This quote from Mahatma Gandhi always resonates with me as it is so true. You come up with this great idea and go along and talk to whoever you think should be interested. At first it is almost impossible to get a meeting; when you do they laugh 'it's been tried before', 'this company will never implement it'. If you persist, the next stage is to argue you down, and sometimes try to besmirch your character or your capabilities. Lastly if you carry on persisting it becomes 'their baby', particularly if it is successful. Then they want the glory!

Anyway back to the story: I got back to the UK and tried the idea out. I ran a whole series of workshops, put in place a front line communication programme, and within two weeks the idea had got traction; within two months it had been implemented and the company reaped the benefits. This was something that I had never experienced before – success on a grand scale. Clearly there was something about this technique, and so the kernel of my approach was born.

There have been a number of initiatives that have adopted this bottom up approach – most notably Jack Welsh's Workout™ programme that revolutionised GE in the USA in the late 1980s. The difference was that most of these were tactical initiatives, looking at incremental changes rather than the radical change which was very much my focus. I wanted to bring a degree of radicalism into Innovation, to look at how companies could bring new concepts into reality.

This book is the story of my journey through the landscape of Innovation: what lessons have been learned, the pitfalls, the successes and the achievements, and more importantly the failures! For many years I continued to develop my ideas and kept trying new concepts, new techniques, new models, until one day on an executive development programme at the Henley Management Centre in the UK, someone asked me; what I thought at the time was a stupid question: 'Ok, so if you've had all this experience, how do *I* do Innovation – how can my company make it a reality?' I was taken aback. Wasn't it obvious? Well, clearly it wasn't.

So I decided to write a simple, foolproof approach to Innovation, and I sat down and developed the 10-step concept. Just the act of writing it down made me reflect on my life and the journey I had taken since my first foray into Innovation way back in 1994. For me it was an amazing time. I know that people say that just before you die your whole life flashes before you – well I was experiencing this without the terminal ending!

So the concept of the 10-step approach was born – a way to turn an organisation inside out. Before I could turn this concept into a reality, I had to wait another couple of years for all the pieces to fall into place. The outcome of all this activity, information gathering and knowledge acquisition coupled with running hundreds of workshops for a wide and diverse range of companies on an eclectic range of topics, is this book, the *10 Steps to Innovation Heaven* – creating true Innovation that really makes a difference, that sticks!

But does it work? Well, I have used the technique over the last few years in a number of companies, and yes the technique does work. It helps bring together the seemingly disparate elements of Innovation into a practical, cohesive framework that can be easily implemented. Each of the elements of the 10-step approach can also be used individually and separately, and this will be discussed at the end of each chapter in more detail.

So why this book and why now? Well I had a burning desire to pass on what I had learned and experienced. I know it sounds bit trite but it is true – I had this 'thing' inside me just waiting to burst out. As with many people I had always dreamed and talked about writing a book. I had the title in 2003 but, also like many people, did nothing about it. Then, just before I was due to take early retirement, I was speaking at a conference and the person next to me at dinner told me she had a book launch the following Wednesday: would I like to come? I mentioned that I had always wanted to write a book, she said 'Come along and I will introduce you to my publisher' – and the rest is history!

Chapter 2

Step 1. What is this thing called Innovation?

My Innovation journey first started, purely by accident, way back in 1994 when I wrote a paper on the 'Impact of technology' for the organisation I worked for – a large government-owned company. Little was I to know what impact this one event would have on my life. The journey has been one that has had many ups and downs, a roller-coaster ride – a journey on which, once started, there has been no going back.

Being immersed in Innovation seems to change your whole outlook on life and even the very way you think, act and behave. For myself it ended in a divorce, periods of frustration and despair, and ultimately the development of a whole new and exciting life; this is not uncommon and there are many examples of colleagues and others who have gone through the same experiences.

It's not that Innovation itself is destructive; it is more that working in this area opens your eyes, gives you confidence and a whole new perspective on the world. It is an incredibly liberating experience which changes you, your values and your life. But as I stated previously, once you have opened this particular Pandora's box, this is a one-way journey and there is no going back!

When I first had the 'magic word' Innovation in my job title back in 1996, I – like everybody else who is catapulted into this situation – was unsure about what it meant. However it was just 'cool' to have this title as Innovation Manager. I couldn't wait to get the business cards – pretty sad!

Most of my career had been in large, traditional companies that operated under what were actually 1980s business models, and this tainted my view of Innovation. I thought that it was just about having great ideas – about being disruptive, being different.

Although Innovation encompasses all these elements there is much more to it than that. However as I hadn't realised that yet, I developed an innate ability to generate new ideas – whether people wanted them or not. I went on every creative thinking course there was, and when I exhausted them I started developing my own creativity tools and techniques (see Appendix 4). This last activity became a little bit of an obsession which resulted in my becoming very disruptive within the organisation. I found myself being ostracised as I kept wanting to tell people about the latest obscure technique I had dreamt up. I took to taking a notepad to bed with me so that great idea at 4 am in the morning – the one we all have at times – wasn't lost. In short I became an Innovation bore, or should that be whore?

However in these early years I was also fortunate enough to be part of a team led by a particularly insightful leader who was excellent at creating the 'right environment', an environment where people could flourish. The team cleared the way and encouraged 'difference' in what was a very staid and traditional company.

This turned out to be one of the most rewarding and exciting periods of my life – being given the opportunity to be 'me' as well as having the freedom and flexibility to do what I thought was right for the company. It is so rare to find leadership that will give people space, allow them to flourish. This experience coloured my view of management and leadership and has given me a model to work to, although I have not found such a rewarding environment again.

One of the ideas I had at the time was that I wasn't going to find the answer to my company's problems within the company itself; if I was going to find answers I would have to look outside. Being part of a large company gave me the freedom to work with other organisations, so I spent around 60 per cent of my time working with other large companies and institutions, focussing on their problems, issues and strategies. Many of these organisations were customers of my company and one of the insights – even at this early stage – was that when we did this 'Innovation stuff' with them it usually resulted in something very positive of some kind, whether that be a new contract, an improved relationship or new business opportunity. At the time we didn't fully recognise what we had discovered; however, more of that later.

Working with this disparate and sometimes eclectic mix of companies brought me some unique insights into other people's and companies' problems. So, 60 per cent of my time I was working outside the company and the other 40 per cent I spent working within it – bringing back the concepts and ideas, and evangelising what I had learned through whatever channel I could find. I didn't realise it at the time but this was truly a unique opportunity. I gained a very broad understanding of a wide range of industries and sectors, and even today I recall lessons and insights learned during that time as well as the many and varied contacts I made.

All this activity was around 1997 and the world around us was changing significantly. The advent of the Internet and the World Wide Web was bringing Innovation into reality – Innovation was happening all around us and we had not noticed.

I felt passionately that the Internet and all it meant was going to radically change the world we lived in, so I embarked on a crusade to tell everybody I came in contact with how important these things would be for us. Unfortunately it was as if I was from another planet. I seemed to be preaching against the 'bible', disturbing the status quo.

At the time I was reading one or two personal development books and I came across that great line from Mahatma Gandhi which I quoted earlier.

'First they ignore you, then they laugh at you, then they fight you, then you win'

'First they ignore you.' This is exactly what was happening to me. I just couldn't seem to get my point across. I was seeing all this innovation and how technology was set to change all our lives, and nobody wanted to listen. I would struggle to get myself a slot on various management team and project meetings to talk about the latest things I had seen and the insights I had on my travels – when I walked into a room it would go silent. People listened politely to my presentation and then I would be dutifully dismissed. After a while this became very disheartening, and at times I felt like giving up. However I believed so strongly that the things I was seeing would have such a major effect on the world, and more particularly on my company, that it was clear to me that it was my 'duty' to persevere.

The media at the time had been quite dismissive about the Internet and were reporting it as a short-lived phenomenon. However it soon became evident that this was not the case and that things were going to be very different in the world of communications. As for me, rather than forcing myself on people I started being invited to speak – in fact it got so bad that I had to ration the number of meetings I attended.

Although the attendance at meetings increased it was still quite adversarial. What the people really wanted was to argue their point, prove I was wrong and try to stop the disruptive 'virus' I was spreading.

Clearly just talking about what was happening or what was about to happen wasn't enough. Somehow I wasn't getting my point across – how could I? For many people what I was talking about was alien: I was speaking a different language of HTTP, IP protocols, FTP, VPN, WWW. They had not seen or heard of anything like the Internet before so they couldn't envisage what it was – or more importantly what it was going to be. What I was seeing in the 'outside' world was something of fundamental importance to the company, but my enthusiasm and excitement were clouding my ability to get my point across – a real learning point for me. Although my enthusiasm was infectious I needed to learn to speak slowly and in a language people could understand!

As my 'popularity' within the company increased I gathered a small team of people around me, because trying to convert what was a large bureaucratic company was impossible as a singleton. After many months we finally persuaded the company to invest in a technology showcase, which we called the Innovation Lab, as a place where we could actually show people what was happening – make it real for people.

The Innovation Lab was to be a purpose-built environment where we could show people the wonders of the new technology-enabled world and the ways people were using it. As well as showing them all this new and sparkly stuff we needed to make sure we got something out of them – it shouldn't be a one-way exchange. We decided to capture their ideas on how the company could respond to these new technologies and techniques, and how it could make use of some of them. I was charged with leading the design initiative and was given a free rein on how it should look and feel. I had been interested in the whole concept of creative thinking for a couple of years – particularly how technology could support the creative process – and so I added a creativity lab (further details of the Innovation Lab are contained in Step 3).

The Innovation Lab was designed to be somewhere where people could have ideas easily, a place which was 'friction free' when it came to people having ideas and developing concepts – somewhere where all the things that stopped people being able to 'free-flow' and be creative had been thrown aside. In this new environment we generated over 200,000 new ideas in two years. How many of these had a tangible positive effect on the bottom line – 5 per cent, 10 per cent? Well actually less than 0.000035 per cent – in fact seven!

So what did we do wrong? We had taken our concept of Innovation and honed it to perfection. We had become great at it – whatever 'it' was. Unfortunately we had forgotten, or not discovered, the most important part of the equation: that an idea is of little use unless something comes of it – the exploitation bit.

An idea is not of 'significant value' unless it is turned into something that has a positive effect on the company/individual/service. We had failed to define what Innovation actually was, what the company meant when it talked about Innovation, what we were actually being asked to do. We didn't have clarity the concept or what an innovative idea would look like, or how we would know if we had had one. In short we had failed – or had we?

I believe we had learned, like Edison and numerous others, the many ways in which Innovation won't work in large companies. The first lesson in Innovation therefore, and the first of my steps, is to define what *you* mean by Innovation.

Define what you mean by Innovation. How will you or your company define it?

You have to understand where you are trying to get to, what the destination will be. How will you know when you have arrived? What will be different, how will things change and how will you measure success? How will it feel and what will life be like?

In *Alice's Adventures in Wonderland,* Lewis Carroll presents an interesting view on understanding the *destination* in a conversation between the Cheshire cat and Alice:

> 'Would you tell me, please, which way I ought to go from here?'
> 'That depends a good deal on where you want to get to,' said the Cat.
> 'I don't much care where –' said Alice.
> 'Then it doesn't matter which way you go,' said the Cat.

Many companies are like Alice. This is particularly the case in modern business with the massive changes that are being seen in terms of globalisation, technological revolution, regulation and competition, as well as the shift in power from supplier to customer and the move to lifestyle marketing. Leaders in the companies know they have to change, they know that they have to 'go somewhere', to do something to respond to these disruptive changes in their environment – but have little clarity of where 'somewhere' is. So they set off on a journey.

As they have little understanding of where they are trying to get to – and even less understanding of what it would be like if they arrived – they are frequently disappointed with the destination when they get there. Although this almost serendipitous strategy can pay off in some cases – particularly if the company is flexible and responsive to new environmental and business stimulus – the leaders are too likely to ignore the 'big picture' and resort to the norm, pursuing a strategy of cost management, constant reorganisation and change. Never mind the strategy, count the paperclips!

So what *is* this thing called Innovation?

A search on the Internet brought up 11.8 million pages that contain the words 'Innovation' and 'definition'. Does this mean that there are 11.8 million definitions? Well no – but there are many hundreds of definitions, each contextually correct but all slightly different. The question is which one is right for you?

In 2005 the EU published a 20-page report that undertook a 'Comparative assessment' of Innovation definitions – including a comparison between the EU, OECD and USA from a 'government' perspective. So what is the answer? What do the experts say? The accepted dictionary definition is:

1. The act of introducing something new.
2. Something newly introduced.

or:

The process of making changes to something established by introducing something new.

This second definition suggests that Innovation is only about improving something that already exists and precludes completely new ideas and concepts. The earliest definition of Innovation I can find comes from Joseph Schumpeter's 1934 book *The Theory of Economic Development*, where he discusses business cycles. It relates to economic innovation but has some interesting parallels with many other definitions:

1) The introduction of a new good – that is one with which consumers are not yet familiar – or of a new quality of good. 2) The introduction of a new method of production, which need by no means be founded upon a discovery scientifically new, and can also exist in a new way of handling a commodity commercially. 3) The opening of a new market, that is a market into which the particular branch of manufacture of the country in question has not previously entered, whether or not this market has existed before. 4) The conquest of a new source of supply of raw materials or half-manufactured goods, again irrespective of whether the source already exists or whether it has first to be created. 5) The carrying out of the new organisation of any industry, like the creation of a monopoly position (for example through trustification) or the breaking up of a monopoly position.

Other definitions include:

- Introduction of a new idea into the marketplace in the form of a new product or service or an improvement in organization or process.
- A new idea, method or device. The act of creating a new product or process. The act includes invention as well as the work required to bring an idea or concept into final form.
- Creating value out of new ideas, new products, new services or new ways of doing things.
- A novel, beneficial change in art or practice.
- The process of converting knowledge and ideas into better ways of doing business or into new or improved products and services that are valued by the community.
- The act of introducing something new and significantly different.
- The process of adopting a new thing, idea, or behaviour pattern into a culture.
- Doing new things.

You can see from the above that the definition is very subjective. All these definitions are possibly and even probably correct for the environment or situation defined and used in. However many people take just one and assume that it is correct for them and more importantly that it is the only one!

When I first started in Innovation, I tried many definitions in an attempt to gain 'traction' within the company. These included 'something that creates chaos', 'a disruptive change', 'having great ideas' and – the one I liked the best – 'the sand in the corporate oyster', irritating it until it produces a 'pearl' of an idea. Clearly none of these were accurate: none of them defined Innovation well enough – all of them were about creativity and crucially missed out the deployment phase of the activity. After several years of repeatedly trying the many definitions of Innovation on initiatives within my own company and within many others, I settled on my own definition, which looking back was a significant turning point:

Innovation = Invention + Exploitation

OK, so this is not revolutionary – but it changed my view and the whole activity of the Innovation team. It gave equal importance to both the exploitation of the ideas and the generation of them. Over time the emphasis changed in favour of exploitation, which brought in new people, new skills, new contacts and a new energy to Innovation within the company. This change brought the team closer to the organisation. For those engaged in the activity, that was a very positive thing – although I am not sure that the organisation knew what had hit it!

What is the difference between creativity and Innovation?

Is creativity the same thing as Innovation? As I mentioned previously, when I first started in this area I thought they were the same – Innovation was creativity and vice versa. What I learned was that they were two very different things, albeit closely linked. Creativity is a skill that can be taught but it requires you to learn a new attitude. Innovation uses the same learned attitude to allow you to control or ignore your self-limiting belief system (an internal control mechanism which we have developed to tell ourselves what we can and cannot do). This new attitude, which you can apply innovatively to your knowledge and experience, comes from the journey of self-discovery that you will get from this book; hopefully you will see things differently, question the status quo and challenge the norm. At times this will be uncomfortable – but if you continue to explore the boundaries of you're self-limiting beliefs though challenge, very quickly you will break them down and start to experience the true joys of Innovation and creativity.

I have learned the hard way that Innovation cannot be taught in its own right. I can give you models and frameworks but it is an intangible thing and relies very much on your approach to life, your attitude, the way you view things and what you know and have learned. So for example, anyone can produce a new design for a window – you don't need to know about building construction or even the laws of physics to be able to do it. I can show you more than 100 techniques that can help stimulate new ideas about its shape, colour, texture and form. To make it a reality, however, can then take you into the realms of Innovation by taking an 'end state', an outcome – the shape and form of the window – and using your knowledge of building, materials (glass, plastic etc.) and maybe even physics to find new ways of creating the window and installing it in a building.

One of the best examples I have come across of Innovation in action is a UK-based lingerie supplier who was having problems selling women's bras over the Internet. I didn't realise but each bra manufacturer has different 'forms' and therefore each range of bras has differently shaped cups and other elements. Unless customers know the manufacturer well they are unlikely to buy something that they can't try on – a big problem with Internet shopping.

The owner of the company was out shopping with his wife in a local supermarket one day and noticed that avocados were packaged in 'blister packs' – thin plastic packaging formed to the rough shape of the avocado. He had the idea that if he could get similar shapes made for all the bra types and sizes, he could send them out to the prospective customer and she could try them on to see which suited her shape the best. This was a cheap and simple solution to a very complex problem. The result was that his online bra sales doubled in the first month and have continued to grow.

In this example the owner had built a link from his problem of selling bras online to retail packaging of fruit and vegetables – he had been a true innovator. Would this idea ever have got through the corporate Innovation process? I think not. It would be too frivolous and probably seen as another 'crackpot' idea. I can hear them say 'We don't do avocados!' The ability to build these tenuous links requires permission to be granted not only to individuals involved in the Innovation initiatives but to the whole organisation.

So are there different types of Innovation?

Innovation can be spelt with a capital 'I' or small 'i'. So what's the difference? you ask. This is again one of the problems with Innovation: it can be all things to all people. Innovation with a small 'i' to me means incremental changes – small step changes in an existing product, service or process, such as a better mousetrap or a new type of gearbox in a car – whereas Innovation with a big 'I' is typically seen as major step change or new and radical thought. It means things like the jet engine, even the Dyson vacuum cleaner or blister pack bra moulds: things that fundamentally change what is already there or introduce something new into the equation.

Most organisations seem to opt for the former as it is less disruptive, and there have been a whole host of programmes sold by consultancies to meet this need to find incremental improvement. The quality movement (total quality management) was developed in the mid-1940s by Dr W. Edward Deming, who at the time was an advisor in sampling at the Bureau of Census and later became a professor of statistics at the New York University Graduate School of Business Administration. TQM was focussed on the quality aspects of a company and looked to improve the overall capability. A follow-on from this work was the concept of quality circles where small groups of employees would meet periodically to try and improve a particular area or process. Jack Welsh in the 1980s again built on this work and developed the Workout process in which the people doing the job eliminate the things that don't add any value – the things that have probably been done in the past, perhaps as a trial or for quality reasons, and have never been taken out.

All these initiatives look to find the 'low-hanging fruit', 'quick wins' – typically targeting frontline staff and looking for easy changes which could transform they way these people work – with massive bottom-line impact. Many of these techniques are still used effectively today by major organisations. They are gaining real bottom-line impact from a large number of small incremental initiatives, implemented by the front line – those who actually do the work. They take activities and work out of the day-to-day job, improving the way the company operates.

Other small 'i' initiatives would include customer first, business process re-engineering and many others – usually fostered by the major consultancies. They all purport to be the magic bullet that will sort out all the company's problems. Many large organisations tend to follow the herd and put their staff through a series of major, typically expensive, initiatives aimed at company turnaround and culture change. The reality is that very few of these initiatives actually deliver on their promise, but they consume large quantities of management and staff time. Not that they don't come up with some great ideas, but it is getting the ideas actually implemented which always causes the problem. On the day, everybody is excited about whatever it is, but then people go back into the corporate treacle and the immune system folds around them and stifles any change.

There is a great diagram I use to describe these activities. It is based on a technology adoption model from the Gartner Group back in the late 1990s. It talks about the wave of hype. A typical quote I have heard time and time again from a senior manager is 'This is going to be the initiative/programme that solves all our problems.' This wave of optimism then transmutes to a trough of despair – 'This will never deliver' – and finally migrates to the plateau of productivity; this is where the initiative actually starts to pay off and the benefits are realised.

The problem in many companies is that when they get to the trough of despair they cut the programme and look to find the next hype wave to hang their hat on to solve all the problems again. Each new initiative starts from scratch with a great wave of hype: 'This new initiative will provide the company with the tools to create the future it needs to survive in the new environment.' Of course the new initiative is only as good as all the other initiatives that have gone before, and soon despair yet again rears its ugly head and the search goes on for the next initiative that is going to solve the company's problems. The plateau of productivity is never actually reached – new initiatives cancel out all the good work that has gone before.

Interestingly if the programme is left to run, usually in the background with a few dedicated individuals, then the benefits are realised. Unfortunately the company is on to the next 'big thing' and

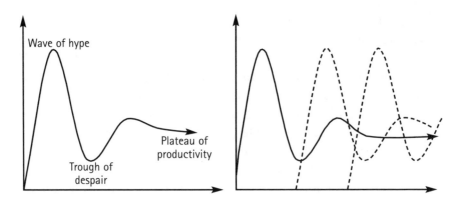

Figure 1 Waves of hype

therefore the significant benefits to the company that some of these initiatives can deliver are not realised or appreciated.

Professor Bainbridge puts the actions down to herd behaviour:

> Is it possible that rational managers would chase fads? Herd behaviour, which refers to the tendency to imitate the actions of others, ignoring one's own information and judgment with regard to the merits of the underlying decision, provides an answer. Corporate managers are scarcely immune to herd behaviour; to the contrary, the faddish aspects of participatory management suggest the possibility that herd behaviour is relevant to the demand side of the equation. ...
>
> Herd behaviour is partly attributable to cognitive biases, especially the conformity effect. When one's decisions are publicly observable by peers, conformity has a positive psychic pay off, whose existence has been experimentally demonstrated.

These are brilliant observations. I might have said the exact same thing, though maybe not as eloquently, but Professor Bainbridge (www.professorbainbridge.com) beat me to it!

Richard T. Pascale from Harvard produced a plot of the initiatives from the late 1800s to late 1995, looking at all the 'silver bullet' initiatives that large organisations signed up to. What was interesting was not only that the growth in these initiatives was phenomenal (and closely correlated with the growth of the consultancies) but also that the initiatives repeated themselves on a four or five-year cycle under a slightly different name. It is not clear whether this reflects the change in the individuals in the top team who buy these types of services or whether organisations have a short memory and can't remember the results the last time they put people through the initiative. I have a dream to update this Pascale's plot one day and see what the impact of management fads has been since 1995 (and whether this correlates to the growth in consultancies and their income!)

Big I Innovation

When we look at Innovation with a big 'I', it seems that there is very little of it in large organisations – in fact I would argue that large

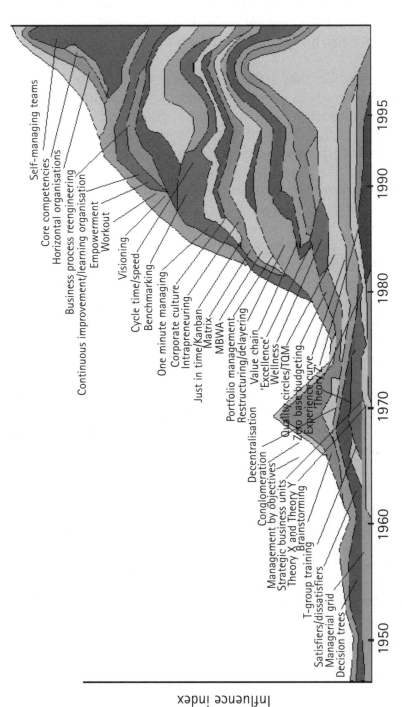

Self-managing teams
Core competencies
Horizontal organisations
Business process reengineering
Continuous improvement/learning organisation
Empowerment
Workout
Visioning
Cycle time/speed
Benchmarking
One minute managing
Corporate culture
Intrapreneuring
Just in time/Kanban
Matrix
MBWA
Portfolio management
Restructuring/delayering
Value chain
'Excellence'
Wellness
Quality circles/TQM
Zero base budgeting
Experience curve
Theory Z
Decentralisation
Conglomeration
Management by objectives
Strategic business units
Theory X and Theory Y
Brainstorming
T-group training
Satisfiers/dissatisfiers
Managerial grid
Decision trees

1950   1960   1970   1980   1990   1995

Influence index

Figure 2 Pascale's plot of management initiatives through the twentieth century

organisations can not be Innovative with a big 'I'. Most of this kind of Innovation is found in small start-ups, or among renegade groups in large companies that have been left alone for a while, isolated from the corporate process and procedures either through ignorance or inefficiency – but seldom by design.

The main reason for this lack of big 'I' Innovation seems to be that its disruptive impact is too great for many companies to bear, and hence there appears to be an inherent 'immune system' that develops within the company to prevent big 'I' Innovation happening – stopping the company from changing too radically and thereby maintaining the status quo. It appears that the only exception to this is where there is some significant external stimulus; a major market or environmental change. Here again it is typically about incremental change with a small 'i' rather than true Innovation with a big 'I'.

An example is Nokia, whose roots go back to the year 1865 with the establishment of a forestry company in southwestern Finland. The year 1898 witnessed the foundation of Finnish Rubber Works Ltd, and in 1912 Finnish Cable Works began operations. Gradually, the ownership of these three companies began to shift into the hands of just a few owners. Finally, in 1967, they were merged to form the Nokia Corporation.

At the beginning of the 1980s, Nokia strengthened its position in the telecommunications and consumer electronics markets through the acquisition of Mobira, Salora, Televa and Luxor of Sweden. In the late 1980s, it became the largest Scandinavian information technology company through the acquisition of Ericsson's data systems division.

Since the beginning of the 1990s, Nokia has concentrated on its core business, telecommunications, by divesting its information technology and basic industry operations. This was not a rapid change and was more of an evolution than a revolution and more of a small 'i' innovation – although if viewed from the present the change looks massive – although it took nearly 30 years.

Big 'I' Innovation, sometimes called radical Innovation, is typically led or pushed by entrepreneurs or people with an entrepreneurial approach, as they usually have a vested interest in making something happen. It is unusual for large organisations to employ these sorts of people, and if they do they usually get sidelined into some backwater, as they are too disruptive to the mainstream operation. They don't fit into the corporate mould and therefore are disruptive to the 'norm'. I have come across many of this type of person in my career and they either become so frustrated that they go through a whole host of jobs – in my case 20 jobs in 14 years – or leave and set up on their own. Unfortunately the company loses their valuable skills.

Big 'I' innovation: something that is based on a markedly different technology or idea

Most big 'I' Innovation, then, seemingly comes from small companies or entities rather than big corporations: somebody has a great idea, a passion, and turns it into a reality, and with luck is then bought out by one of the big companies. The 1990s was the most successful period for this type of 'transition' from idea to initial public offering. Unfortunately many of these ideas were just that: ideas. When the new owner tried to commercialise them there wasn't a market, they didn't work or they were just not appropriate!

This is the history of the Internet bubble. The guy with the vision sold out and went and lay on a beach somewhere, and the company that had bought it was left with a lemon – a product or service which just wasn't viable.

An example is where one major electronics company decided it needed to inject some new ideas, products, and life into the company so it went on a fairly aggressive acquisition campaign – buying four Internet-based companies, which were reasonably successful in their own right, for many millions of pounds. The electronics company had a policy of buying the leader/founder of the companies out so it could manage the new enterprises to maximum growth. What actually happened was that once the founder went, the companies and staff got assimilated within the parent company within two months – and lost their drive, their identity and their passion. The people from the smaller company craved stability and structure, and soon adopted the parent company frameworks and, interestingly, the culture. The parent company had paid a huge amount of money for actually very little. Clearly the corporate immune system had worked overtime to prevent this 'Innovation virus' attacking the organisation.

Little 'i' innovation

One fun way of understanding what your company is about is to play Innovation bingo (see Figure 3). This is an extension of 'bullshit bingo', which has been around since the late 1980s where you mark off your bingo card in meetings and other occasions with the words appearing on the card, and when you get a line or the four corners or whatever, you shout bingo. This is great fun for the participants although it can be a little disturbing for the presenter – especially if he/she doesn't know what is happening! Innovation bingo runs along the same lines but uses a different set of words to find out if the language of your company is Innovative with a small 'i' or Innovative with a big 'I'. Although this probably won't help you with your plans for Innovation it will give you a sense of the challenges you will face ahead; if the language is small 'i' then your approach will need to be very different from what you would use if it was big 'I'. In a small 'i' organisation, it is highly unlikely that you can achieve a revolution, although the evolutionary approach of incremental change will be easier.

Groundswell

The question in this small 'i' scenario is: 'Can you create enough small changes to create a *groundswell* of change and thereby achieve relatively radical Innovation – almost by stealth?' In a big 'I' organisation, if there is such a thing, making the small incremental changes will be difficult. However a structured approach using one of the defined methodologies such as Workout could provide a way of helping the big thinkers focus on the low-hanging fruit. One interesting question is whether there is an innovation lifecycle. In other words do companies go through cycles of big 'I' Innovations and then a whole series of small 'i' 'ripples' follow – refining the original concept until a the next big 'I" wave is needed?

I hope you can see that the delineation between incremental and radical Innovation is one of the first things that you need to decide on before you start on your Innovation journey. What are you trying to achieve? When I work with companies on defining their Innovation initiatives the first thing I like to do is to get the senior management team to visualise how things would be in the new Innovative

Creative	Facilitate	Flexibility	Brainstorm	Solve	Action	Forecast	Process	Outline	Results
Provocative	Strategic	Entrepreneur	Pro-active	Extrapreneur	Analysis	Value	Assessment	PRINCE	Discipline
Scenario	Fun	Understand	Goal	Invent (ion)	Capability	Timescale	Attitude	Profile	Resource
Adapt	Team	Action	Immerse	Radical	Time-out	Long-term	Objective	Quality	Purpose
Innovate	Lead	Navigate	Portfolio	Idea	Plan	Task	Park that	Incremental	Mission
Creation	Define	Target	Purpose	Vision	Improve	Extend	Target	Conventional	Communicate
Communication	Leadership	Fuzzy	Accountability	Goal	Power	Translate	Define	Reinforce	Solid
Open	Paradigm	Dysfunctional	Wisdom	Observable	Results	Scorecard	Reason	Foundation	Responsibility
Big picture	Knowledge	Ethical	Synergy	Team dynamics	Perform-ance	Measure-ment	Feedback	Outcome	Frequency
Possible	Radar	Empowered	Global	Adaptive	Baseline	Downsize	Information	Problem	Cohesive
Future	Radical	Environment	Expansive	Challenge	Quarterly	Mastery	Architecture	Approve	Re-engineer

Figure 3 Innovation bingo

First 5 words on either side define whether you are in a 'BIG I' (Innovation) meeting or a 'little i' (incremental) meeting – be careful, some words appear on both sides

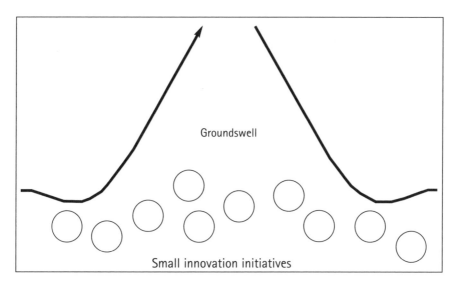

Figure 4 Groundswell of change

Company. Imagine it is five years in the future and the Innovation initiative has been the most successful programme the company has ever embarked on:

- What would customers be saying?
- What would the shareholders/market be saying – how would they be reacting?
- What would the press be saying about the company and what it was achieving?
- What would a day be like in the life of one of the senior management team?
- How would it feel to be part of it?

* * *

The importance of understanding the destination cannot be stressed enough. In Step 1 we have looked at why it is important and how you can start to define what it should be. I have provided a number of tools and techniques that will hopefully help you formulate your ideas, creating a compelling vision for your company – or yourself. The techniques discussed are just as valid for your personal life as they are for your business life: creating a compelling vision for yourself energises your activities and provides a focus for your life. Start your own journey today!

Chapter 3

Step 2. Understanding where you are – and how to change

We saw in the previous chapter the importance of understanding where you are trying to get to, what you are trying to achieve and how you will know when you get there. However, before you set off on any journey it is important that you understand where you are starting from. This is a step that very few organisations actually undertake when embarking on something new. They very often start Innovation initiatives without that understanding, and 18 months down the line are invariably disappointed that things haven't changed and nothing has been achieved. One of the defining features of an innovative organisation is its culture. This is something that is seldom written down and is typically passed down the organisation through a series of stories that define the organisation and its behaviour – what is acceptable, what is not, how the organisation operates and what is tolerated. So part of this step is to try and understand the culture of the organisation.

This realisation led me into a whole new field of research, which looked at how these stories are created, disseminated and interpreted. If the day-to-day life of the organisation is governed by these stories, can you tell something about how Innovative the organisation is through them? More interestingly can you change the culture of the organisation, and its Innovative capability, by 'seeding' stories?

In 2003 I interviewed a number of senior managers within the company on the subject of storytelling and its power to influence the culture of the organisations. The managers thought that although they had never tried it, it would certainly be possible to influence the culture of the company in this way. Most agreed that actually this was probably the real essence of leadership. The profile of a leader, or indeed a manager, is created through stories about their past, about their actions and their deeds. Good leaders seemed to create their own stories, their own legends. Unfortunately storytelling in business has declined in popularity as it has had bad press through its overuse by political parties who have used the technique and 'spun' stories to try and gain an edge and have to some degree discredited the 'technique'. However it is still a powerful tool in an Innovator's armoury and should be considered early in any Innovation initiative:

- What stories do you want people to tell?
- How would these stories help your initiative?
- What would happen if the wrong stories were being told?
- What channels are available to seed these stories?
- Who do people listen to?

So how do you start to understand how Innovative you are as an individual and as an organisation? There are many methods that can be adopted and many consultancies that will offer to do it for you. When I was leading a large Innovation team, we realised that our efforts to achieve the organisation's goals for the Innovation initiative were hampered by an inherent lack of understanding about the Innovation journey. Initially we were pretty much left alone to set our own targets, and we tried many of the classic metrics – primarily taken from Innovation in product companies, although we did invent some of our own which were a bit obscure and didn't last long. As the company I was involved in was a service industry, many of these metrics taken from product or research-led companies were irrelevant or ineffective in our industry.

If we look at how Innovation is typically implemented within organisations, there are three areas where measurement can be undertaken: the *process* of Innovation itself, the *output* from Innovation activities and lastly the *consequences* of any Innovation activity. If the objective is just to have more ideas, then it may be best to measure output or process. If the objective were to change the culture of the organisation, then process and consequence would be more relevant.

The last of the three, although it does not lend itself to measurement easily, is the one that most clearly indicates whether Innovation is

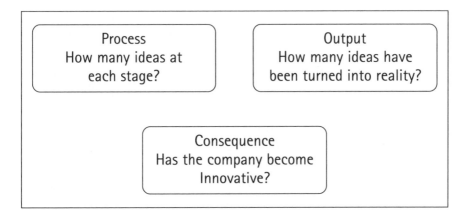

Figure 5 Process, output and consequence

endemic within the company. Has viral Innovation become a reality? This is something that I believe many organisations would wish to achieve and are aiming at, but without a framework they fail to achieve it. The output and process can easily be measured, as there are tangible things that can be counted – things that can be seen and felt – and these are loved by the finance function, whereas consequences are more difficult to measure as the criteria relate to people's attitude, behaviour, activity and to some degree ability. The area of measurement and benchmarking is discussed in more detail in Chapter 11.

The methodology we adopted to measure the consequential output was simple: ask people within the company how innovative they thought they and the company were. The idea of focus groups was mooted for a while, but the cost and complexity of organising this on a large scale made it prohibitive. Our solution was to put together an online survey – an Innovation audit – which was circulated to a large population of managers across the company. In his book *The Wisdom of Crowds*, James Surowiecki talks about the use of a large group to set corporate strategy and company direction. We used a similar technique to gauge the innovation temperature of the company through the use of online tools and techniques.

To develop the survey, we looked at similar types of activities undertaken by large consultancies, talked to a number of academic establishments and distilled what we thought was going to be the most effective set of questions out of all our research and experience. The survey was undertaken using a web-based survey tool (www.facilitate.com) so the distribution costs were negligible, and the response was higher than expected at 30 per cent (typical printed surveys have a response of less than 10 per cent). The survey purposely focussed on the negatives, what was stopping Innovation happening, rather than the positives – what was helping Innovation occur – as we wanted to find what the barriers were and thereby minimise their effect.

The survey we used is contained in Appendix 1 and on www.sticky innovation.com website for you to complete yourself. This will allow you not only to understand your particular Innovation index score but also to measure your company's score against others.

The insights from the survey within my company were that the organisation did not appear to have an Innovative/Innovation culture even though we had been working to try and promote it for more than five years. The results of the survey showed that there were many factors that were hindering innovation in the company – some of them tangible and some intangible. The survey defined six factors that appeared to be the most significant in stopping an Innovative way of life within the company. The factors were:

- Culture   '... we don't do things like that.'
- History   '... that's not the sort of thing we would get involved in.'
- Permission '... it isn't my job.'
- Space   '... the environment just isn't conducive to thinking.'
- Time   '... I just don't have time to think.'
- Money   '... I don't have any spare money in my budget for new things.'

Many of these things were 'intangible' and were actually self-limiting beliefs, things that the people in the organisation 'thought' rather than 'real world' blockers. This was a revelation to the team as they assumed that the barriers would be much more tangible, things that could actually be addressed – such as the lack of a credible suggestion scheme or lack of clarity of purpose – that are cited by many academics as the true barriers. Clearly the respondents didn't see them as such.

The things that were stopping the organisation being innovative were there in the organisation itself!

OK, so some of the things were tangible, *space, time* and *money*. The company did address these through introducing an Innovation fund, an internal venture capital fund to provide *money*. It built the Innovation Lab to provide *time* and *space* for people to think (these are covered in greater detail in Step 3). Although these did have an effect and stimulated over 160 initiatives, the culture of the organisation didn't fundamentally change and the fund died after 18 months – mainly because effective management metrics hadn't been introduced and proof of value hadn't been achieved.

But what about the intangibles? How could *culture, history* and *permission* be addressed? What actions could be taken to start to address these areas?

As previously mentioned, culture is something that is very intangible – very rarely written down but passed through the organisation by word of mouth and by the actions of those who work in the company. Anthropologists use the term culture to refer to the universal human capacity to classify experiences, and to encode and communicate them symbolically. This makes addressing culture within a company a challenge to say the least. As with Innovation itself, the first step is to understand what changes are required.

- What should the culture be?
- What characterises the culture within the company?
- What are the important components of the culture in your company?
- How would it feel to be part of the company?
- How would people behave if the culture had changed?

Defining this culture in writing is not going to be easy and I can guarantee that whatever is written down will be wrong – or at least not right. One method that has been used with success within the Innovation Labs is to get people to role-play the new culture through a series of workshops. Bearing in mind the concept of *groundswell*, this should be carried out on the outside of the 'hive', as close to the front line of the organisation as possible.

In these workshops, the groups work together to build and role-play the concepts of the new corporate culture based in the values and beliefs the company wants to engender. This is then fed back in a variety of ways, looking at the impact of the new culture from four different perspectives: employee, employer, stakeholder and customer. This technique is one that has been developed for use within the Innovation Labs and is called 'other people shoes' (OPS); it is covered in more detail in Appendix 4.

The stories developed as part of this exercise can be disseminated either through normal company cascade channels, or by using video or podcasts to cascade to teams and managers. It is important that the people doing the cascade have been actively involved in the creation of the stories and therefore have a 'passion' for the subject. Their enthusiasm is important as it lends credibility to the message and helps others understand what is required.

Once you have defined the elements that need to be 'developed' there are a number of techniques that can be employed to create culture change. These are described below.

Communication

Effective communication is vital if you are trying to achieve culture change in the organisation. It is the one thing that not only is relatively easy to do but also has a huge impact on the company, team or individuals. Going back to the bee metaphor I used previously, I call this the 'dance of Innovation', and it is covered in more detail in Step 5. Just as bees will come back to the hive when they have found a new food source and tell the other bees where and how far the food is, so people involved in Innovation come back into the company and tell what new ideas have arisen, what has happened and the effect. This 'dance' gives the rest of the employees permission to act and think differently.

Unfortunately, many organisations rely totally on the company magazine, which is typically full of 'good news' stories mixed with 'death, doom and despondency'. It is written by professional journalists to promote a particular company line – typically 'Don't worry everything is OK' or 'The world is coming to an end as competition eats into our market.' Interviewing frontline staff in a number of companies reveals that there is a great deal of cynicism about these publications; their value in terms of changing culture and so on is very limited.

So what should this 'dance' look like? Well it can take many forms, but the most powerful is when the individuals themselves do the communicating. I have seen several different ways of performing this 'activity', from interviews in external magazines, through videos of whatever the activity is shown at team meeting and other occasions, to individual team presentations and one-to-ones with key influencers. A recent example of how this 'dance' adopts new technologies is the use of video podcasting and webcasting, where individuals have put together a short video that can be transmitted over the Internet or intranet to a wide audience. Although the quality is not great, the passion and the personality certainly come across.

Interviewing people before and after watching such a video, or being exposed to the 'dance' is fascinating, as they feel so much more empowered after seeing what has been done in other parts of the company or in other organisations.

One point to remember here is that although internal communication is very useful, an external interview, press article or media interview is probably five times more valuable – certainly in terms of gaining management support. The added credibility given to external media articles is out of proportion to the effort it takes to create them. The more 'respectable' the publication or programme, the higher is the 'reflected' benefit for the company and senior management. Many companies put a high value on column inches in the broadsheet press. When I contributed to an article on the Innovation Labs for the *Financial Times* I received a letter of congratulations from the CEO; it had taken less than 40 minutes of my time and yet it was mentioned in my annual appraisal and was reflected in my bonus for the year. A totally disproportionate response, but it proved to me the value of external publicity to organisations.

Sociability

The ability to socialise the situation can be highly effective. As mentioned in the previous section on communication, one method is to get people to communicate to a wide audience about the way they have achieved something. Making this communication social is another way of giving people permission in a non-confrontational, 'easy' relaxed atmosphere. So where would such socialisation take place? In the USA, the company picnic used to be the place where employees and their families would gather on an annual basis to 'bond'. However in many other counries this phenomenon never really caught on, and although there have been office 'open days' and 'family days', they are not effective in this context.

A powerful method of socialising the change culture came out of the total quality management activities of the early 1990s. The concept of total quality fairs was employed by a number of companies to promote and disseminate good ideas and best practice across a wide community. When I joined a large UK company in 1989, it was in the throes of the total quality movement. An annual quality fair was held in a central UK location where around 100 'booths' were constructed and manned by extremely enthusiastic people – passionate about whatever it was they had come up with or whatever they were doing. Some of the ideas were extremely simple operational improvements, but one or two had a huge potential payback if implemented company wide. The fair was visited by thousands of people over a period of a week and the buzz this generated was amazing. People were visibly changed by what they saw and experienced. At the time the company ran a rudimentary suggestion scheme, and the number of suggestions rose by a factor of 120 in the three weeks following the event.

Although there was this increase in ideas the real tangible 'value' of the fair could not be adequately measured and the fairs ceased as the company moved on to the next 'big thing' – to process management, business process improvement or investors in people. The cost of staging the event was significant and when looked at in pure balance sheet terms, setting the cost against the benefits such as increased efficiency or increased sales, it was almost impossible to build the linkages between this as a cause and the effect some time later in some obscure part of the company. The intangible value was immense however and the loss of this type of event withdrew an element of 'permission' for people with similar ideas. This of course was never measured and therefore never recognised.

Openness

Tell it like it is! The constant drip feed of good news in typical corporate communication has led to cynicism and the dilution of any message. Many people have become jaded in their view of the 'corporate message'. There needs to be a level of honesty in these communications – where something hasn't worked or hasn't achieved what it was supposed to, then tell people. Don't forget this is contributing to the stories that go to make up the culture of the company, and one of the things that should be promoted is that it is OK to make mistakes – as long as no one gets hurt and there isn't a significant negative financial impact on the company.

The ethos in many companies – certainly in the late 1990s – was that failure was just that: a failure. If an idea was squashed or it just didn't work, then typically the people involved were sidelined or even fired. This sent a message throughout the company that it was definitely not OK to fail, and this stifled any Innovation and ideas.

In the USA there seems to be a different ethos, and failure is actually celebrated in some quarters. Most of the 'big' CEOs in the USA have repeatedly failed at some level within their business careers. This was not seen as failure so much as a learning opportunity to ensure the mistakes never occurred again. A much more positive attitude prevails. Henry Moore, the English sculptor, had a great quote about failure that sums this up perfectly, I believe:

> The secret of life is to have a task, something you bring everything to, every minute of the day for your whole life. And the most important thing is: It must be something you cannot possibly do.

We should all strive to fail but never make the same mistake twice. I must admit to having failed several times in my career, sometimes spectacularly, and rather than seeing these incidents as problems I have tried to use them as a time to reflect and learn from them and I believe I am a better person for having failed.

* * *

In Step 2 we have looked at the importance of understanding where you or your company is today. 'Baselining' your current activities gives you the ability to measure how far you have travelled on your journey. Without this you or your company will always be disappointed, as you will always be fighting the perception that nothing has changed – which unfortunately usually becomes reality in a very short time. Therefore understanding your current state – in all its dimensions, or at least as many as you can realistically find – enables a rational view to be taken and argued when appropriate. As with Step 1 the techniques and approaches are just as valid for you as an individual as for your company. The need to have a clear understanding of your life today allows you to fully appreciate the benefits of embarking on this journey.

Chapter 4

Step 3. Create the right environment

In the previous chapters we have discussed the importance of understanding what you mean by Innovation, the need to define the destination you are trying to get to and the significance of appreciating where you are starting.

In this chapter, the third of the 10 steps, we will look in some detail at how you can create a supportive environment for Innovation to flourish in your company. Although primarily focussed on innovation initiatives within companies, the elements covered in this section are valid for personal as well as company use.

Environment in this context covers many aspects that provide the resources required to make Innovation a reality. This can include the physical environment, funding and people who are involved through to the leadership and management of the activity within the company. I have split this down into what I consider to be the four most important areas:

- physical environment
- people
- leadership
- funding.

They are arranged in no particular order and I leave you to judge their importance in your own specific situation. I have found that all four usually need to be in place for Innovative 'fusion' to occur – self-sustaining organisational Innovation. However I have seen examples where, even though only two or three are in place, successful Innovation has taken place – although its 'stickiness', its sustainability and bottom-line impact, have been diluted to some extent.

Physical environment

This is an area I have become increasingly passionate about over my time working in Innovation. When I first started way back in 1994, I didn't think that *where* you Innovated was important; I thought anywhere was OK. What I have learned is that the physical environment is a very important factor, as it appears to significantly govern people's beliefs and behaviour, and their ability to be creative and Innovative in their thinking.

In 1997 I was asked to put together a technology showcase for the company. At the time I was part of an innovation and futures team within the IT part of the organisation. I had seen some of the things that were happening with the Internet and the World Wide Web and had embarked on a crusade to wake people up to what was happening outside our safe little world. The company was, and still is, a large-scale user of Lotus Notes, which is a centralised email/database system that requires users to replicate their email databases on a regular basis. I was talking about the power of Internet email systems that were truly distributed and required less technical and communication resources. I remember that I received a note from the IT director of one the business units 'forbidding' me 'to speak to anyone' in that unit – a King Canute approach I guess you could call it. I was disrupting the status quo and causing waves in the company – people were becoming dissatisfied and had the gall to ask and expect new things.

As the company was in the communications business, there were things happening outside the organisation that would fundamentally change the market and indeed the business we were in. I likened it to the evolution of mammals and the demise of the dinosaurs – we were trying to be the most efficient dinosaur on the planet and were totally missing the fact that the mammals – the Internet and the competition – were evolving very rapidly all around us.

I had at the time been working on the fringes of creativity with a number of large UK organisations: large financial and FMCG (Fast Moving Consumer Goods) companies. So when I was given the job of designing this technology showcase I decided to add a creativity lab on the back. I had no idea what one should look like but I felt it should be somewhere were people felt safe to think. I came up with the idea of a womb. (I am sure that the psychologists among you could have a field day with this!)

The creativity room, the womb, had soft pink lighting and curvy white walls, very different from anything else in the company, or in the world at the time as we were to find out. To achieve the curvy walls we looked at various materials, and decided on a white laminate that would be the most durable and effective. We discovered that we could write on these walls and that dry-wipe whiteboard pens would rub off – and so the write-on floor-to-ceiling whiteboard was born. Little did we know at the time, but we had embarked on a path that would take us on an amazing journey of discovery and change our lives forever.

The Innovation Lab was born six months after the first idea – a record for the company and a huge personal achievement for the people involved. Nothing of this size had ever been implemented in such a short time and with such an impact on the company. There was something almost spooky about this project. The money was there. We found a location at the company's management training centre in some redundant portable buildings (these had been used as temporary classrooms). The support was there from the management board – everything just seemed to fall into place.

The pilot Innovation Lab was very successful and we developed a way of working along with a whole host of tools and techniques to use within the facility. Over 10,000 people visited the pilot Lab in its two and half years of operation. We had articles in the *Financial Times* and we were mentioned on *Tomorrow's World* (a science programme on the BBC)

The facility was split into four – the technology showcase, the creativity lab, a development lab and an office area. One of our early challenges was how to run such a facility: What would one expect to do in an Innovation Lab? We ended up developing our own way of working, tools, techniques and so on. Many are still in action today in the labs around the UK. We trained over 400 people in 'active facilitation', a style of facilitation developed for use in these creative environments.

Visitors entered the facility through the technology showcase area, which was very dark and atmospheric, and were usually guided through by one of the Future and Innovation team – showing them the latest developments in areas they would be interested in. The concept of storytelling as an active medium for helping people to understand what was being described was developed in the early stages of the Lab, and we realised that the stories we told had persistence that normal PowerPoint presentations didn't have.

At the time, we did some subjective research – giving the same information as a report, a story and a PowerPoint, and then going back on a regular basis to ask people to recount what they remember from the session. More than 30 per cent of the people did not even read the report, the PowerPoint had a persistence of around three to six days, while the story was still remembered up to three months later. This research was extended later to pictures, graphics and other presentations, and will be discussed in more detail later in the book.

One of the most significant features of the Lab, and the mainstay of the facility for the first few years, was the use of technology to support the creative thinking process. I had been working for some time with a contact from a large financial institution that had been experimenting with meeting management software from the University of Arizona. The software, Groupsystems, provided an agenda-based approach to electronic meetings which could be either local or across a network connection (at the time network connections were 'permanent' and very slow so this option was ruled out quite early).

One of the 'features' of the software was that participants could be anonymous. Although this was not used in the normal operation of a meeting, we picked up on this feature as it allowed a level of freedom for participants in the Innovation Lab sessions. The software allowed anonymous brainstorming to take place and the participants could then take the output and group it, vote on it and generally manipulate it – seamlessly. Although not specifically written to support the creative process, this software became a reason for people to use the Lab and was the backbone of many of the sessions that were run within the facility. Similar software is still used in the Innovation Labs today and continues to provide the participants with a 'friction free' environment to generate ideas, build strategies and so on, and generally collaborate in an anonymous and non-threatening way.

The software 'flattened the playing field' as it allowed everyone in the workshop to have the same input to the session. In a company where status was important, this was a great enabler as many of the best ideas came from the junior members of the team or from the clerical support people. The senior guys (it was still a mainly male-dominated management structure) didn't particularly like the anonymity as they couldn't find out who was saying what. However the results were usually so good that they put up with it and actively promoted it.

So back to the Lab. Once they'd had their tour of the technology showcase the visitors would go through to the creativity Lab to brain-storm ideas on how they or their teams could use some of the technology they had seen. The facility was highly productive in terms of the number of ideas, but as mentioned previously it missed out on the implementation part of Innovation. In two years we generated over 168,000 ideas using the software but very few actually 'stuck' and made it into reality. We did develop some tools to harvest these ideas that used technology for clustering them (or using our bee metaphor 'ideas swarming') into similar topics and/or areas.

One thing we noticed was that if we brought people straight into the creativity lab without going through the technology showcase area, the ideas we got were very different; there was something about going through a transition of sorts – moving through an 'alien' environment, leaving the reality of day-to-day business behind – that was changing the way people thought about issues. This triggered the realisation that the environment was in some way conditioning the way people thought.

In 1999 the company decided to set up a new purpose-built facility as the local government planning permission had run out on the current site and the portable buildings had to be removed. Various options were considered, including the idea of putting the facility on a train or an Innovation bus and taking it around the country. All these options were discounted and the business case for the new facility was put in writing – actually a very difficult task, since the costs could be clearly identified whereas the benefits couldn't. Of course our finance colleagues tried in many ways to understand the benefits of the facility, but it comes back to the problem of how to measure the intangible effect of such a facility on the company. I understand much more now how to put together a business case for such a facility, but at the time it was the blind leading the blind!

The final decision to go ahead was given by the CEO of the company personally. He *felt* that the company had to build the new lab – a very intuitive and brave decision, and one that proved right for the organisation at that time.

This new facility gave me the opportunity to explore further my idea that environment conditions thinking, and I got to spend the next six months travelling around the world researching my ideas and thoughts. I visited over 50 locations in the UK, USA and Europe, ranging from similar facilities that had sprung up in major consultancies, funded by a hardware company based in Silicon Valley, through museums and galleries to theme parks such as Disneyland. In many of these locations I asked a standard set of questions and was amazed at the responses I received. There appeared to be a link between their surroundings and the responses I was receiving – people seemed to be taking cues from their environment.

In parallel to this, we ran a whole series of standard workshops back in the UK in various locations such as hotels, meeting rooms, board rooms, training rooms and other 'standard' meeting/workshop locations. What we found was that people behaved differently in each location; they seemed to have a 'learned behaviour' for each and were taking cues from their environment, which was affecting the way they were acting, and the ideas they generated. When challenged, nobody could tell us what these rules were or how they knew which way to behave – they just did! Clearly the rules had been passed on through observation and the ubiquitous storytelling about previous meetings.

In the board room people were very quiet; they talked in hushed voices, and waited for other people to finish before speaking. Their ideas were very 'conservative', typically non-controversial and in-line with the company's norm.

In company meeting rooms a different behaviour was observed. Here there was even a hierarchy of who sat where – something we also observed in the Innovation Lab. The meeting leader would typically sit either at the end of the room furthest from the door or half-way down one of the sides, the person taking the notes or documenting the meeting would sit nearest the door, and so on. People respected the 'structure' and formality of the meeting or workshop, and when asked to rearrange the furniture they resisted quite strongly – they felt comfortable with the familiar.

Even in the Innovation Lab there were set places for different individuals. The senior person in the room always sat opposite the facilitator – I guess vying for dominance – while the secretary or administrative person always sat at the table in front of the facilitator. The 'agent' for the meeting, the person who had set it up, sat at the back next to the door – guarding the exit. We had great fun mixing these people up in sessions and watching their body language and behaviour. I am sure a whole new book could be written on the psychology of this alone.

In a training room, people were happy to sit in a formal arrangement as if at school, and tended to act at times like school children – passing notes and the like. When asked to rearrange the furniture they sought permission from the 'leader', and again seemed quite reluctant to 'own' the space.

In a hotel meeting room the group would be quite passive, and their behaviour depended to some degree on the layout of the room. If the room was laid out with small groups sitting around tables, then there appeared to be one set of behaviour. A hierarchy was quickly established and a table spokesperson emerged, with all comments channelled through that individual. If the tables were set up in a horseshoe then another type of behaviour was exhibited, where there was lots of eye contact before anything was said; people were quieter and more reserved.

In each of the different spaces there seemed to be a set of unwritten rules that were being applied; nobody discussed them but they were clearly there. So when we got round to designing the new Innovation Lab facility, one of the main premises for the design was that the environment should provide no cues on how to behave – and therefore should be less restrictive when it came to creativity and Innovation.

So back to the story and the design of the new Innovation Lab. We had found that people were taking cues from their environment and this was affecting their behaviour – particularly how creative or innovative they were. So the question became:

> How do you build an environment where people don't know how they are expected to think, have no cues to restrict their thought processes?

This led to the facility having curved 'whiteboard' walls, bright primary colours, objects that you wouldn't normally expect to find in an office environment (palm trees and toys, for example) and a layout that you would certainly not find in any organisation. The Innovation Lab opened on 1 April 2000 and is still fully operational today, although its ownership moved from the Innovation and Research team to the Human Resources and Training team in 2004. The Innovation Lab has had more than 20,000 visitors since its opening in 2000, and has generated over 168,000 great ideas, although in reality only a small number generated bottom-line benefit for the company.

The academic community within the UK embraced the concept of the Innovation Lab through the Learning the Habit of Innovation (www.lhi.org) project, and there are at least 11 Innovation labs operational in 2006, with new ones opening every year. A list of all the innovation labs along with contact details is in Appendix 2.

In 2005 the first Innovation lab in a school (Hassenbrook School) was opened with backing from the government. This takes the concept, first developed for business, into an educational environment that is primarily used by 11–14 year olds as part of the UK National Curriculum. The centre has become a model for Innovative teaching practice and there are plans to extend the concept across the UK and Europe. The pupils who use it are highly motivated and find the environment and atmosphere highly conducive to discovery – of themselves and their capabilities.

People

Finding the right people to be involved in Innovation activity is key to its success. Experience has shown that advertising for an

Innovative person just doesn't work. You may get plenty of people applying but unfortunately people's ideas of what an innovative person is are coloured by the perceived glamour of the activity. On numerous occasions over the last 12 years I have recruited people for a role in the Innovation team only to be disappointed by the results. People want the travel, the title, the benefits and of course the glory – but without the hard work, rejection and frustration that goes on behind the scenes.

Finding the right people

So how do you find people who are right? Well typically you don't – they find you!

The best people are the ones that seek you out – their passion and drive shine through. There are many profiling techniques that you can use, and these can be indicators of people's personality and preferences. However when it comes down to it, very often it is gut instinct that prevails. I have recruited individuals who on paper are superb and probably have in their repertoire the ability to 'walk on water'. When we got to working with them, however, there was something missing – some part of their make-up wasn't quite right. I have learned that basic instinct is one of the best factors for knowing whether somebody is right for a job in this area.

Before I moved into the innovation area I remember buying a set of motivational tapes by Brian Tracey, a US management guru. He maintained that in any interview situation you have either got the job or not in the first five minutes – that is how long it takes on average for someone's intuition to click in. In the rest of the interview the interviewer is looking for facts to support his/her decision. I have seen this in action so many times now on both sides of the table, as interviewer and interviewee. It is fascinating observing what is happening on a minute-by-minute basis. I guess I have lost a few jobs this way, but I learned a lot about people.

When we first built the Innovation team in the late 1990s, it was a collection of people who had found each other and sort of coagulated together into a 'team'. Luckily the management at the time saw the opportunities of allowing this grouping to take place – there were interesting team dynamics. Although the members worked together well most of the time, there were periods of extreme angst and conflict. We stumbled across the Myers-Briggs technique of personal preference profiling and were amazed at how much it helped us to get along and understand how each other thought and liked to work.[1]

Typically for an Innovation team we could not go with the norm and developed our own version of it for use with teams in the Innovation Lab environment. However it showed the importance of a good mix of people on the team and reflected the need to have someone who could actually finish something rather than people who just had lots of ideas.

Once you have found a few people who can work together and have complementary characteristics and strengths, the next problems is how to motivate and, more importantly, 'measure' them. If you are in a large organisation you will have to go through the appraisal and objective-setting processes. Traditional objectives and objective-setting processes don't always work: they can be too restrictive for creative and innovative people. The other problem with these types of people is that their approach to their work will be opportunistic, and therefore the objectives may be OK today but be out of date in a month's time. There is a need to have a flexible targeting and objective-setting framework to allow for the discontinuous nature of their work. In my early days, objective setting got to be complicated, so we ended up setting the objectives at the end of the year – and surprisingly I always managed to achieve them!

So once you have a flexible objective-setting and targeting framework in place how do you motivate people to keep battling against the organisation to achieve their Innovation goals. My experience is that there has to be fun – Innovation and creativity utilise the right side of the brain that is stimulated by fun and play. My own take on this is:

'aha! is only one letter away from ha-ha.'

Secondly, there has to be a feeling of value – whatever the individual members are doing needs to be valued by their peers and the organisation or team. This is very important in an environment that is constantly trying to 'kill' whatever you are trying to achieve. Patience, passion and persistence are some of the virtues that all people working in Innovation need to possess in huge amounts to survive, as they will be frustrated and have to face not only work rejection but also personal rejection at times.

Lastly, people need to be rewarded for their efforts; companies very often forget this. Some product companies reward people by allotting a percentage of the profits or revenue, but this is very rare – particularly in service organisations. Where flexible targeting and objective setting are in place, it is important that they reflect what is really happening and are not allowed to lapse, as this can restrict remuneration. Being aware of this is half the battle, as 'special' systems and arrangements can be put in place to make sure that the hard work is rewarded.

One trap related to setting up an Innovation team, which many organisations fall into, is that it becomes the 'answer'. Just as the next initiative is going solve all our problems, so will the creation of an Innovation team. Just by setting up a team, the company/organisation has passed responsibility to somebody or something – it is no longer everyone's job to be Innovative. It is now this team's role. Suddenly, because a team has been set up, the effect that the organisation is trying to gain is quashed.

So how can you get round this problem? Firstly, keep the team very lean – certainly no more than two or three people. Focus their activity on stimulation and leadership rather than on practical ideas generation. Aim for the team to become the centre of a community rather than trying to become the community itself. This will be hard since as the initiative becomes successful, it will become the honey pot and become highly attractive to be part of.

Leadership

One of the key elements of successful Innovation activities within companies is leadership. Leaders need to create the situation and environment for Innovative and creative people to flourish, and more importantly for the whole organisation to become Innovative. This is not an easy task – particularly for today's crop of leaders, focussed on shareholder value, globalisation, competition and the many other issues faced by companies today.

Much has been written about leadership; in fact in 2005 there were over 300 books published on the subject. A search on Amazon results in over 70,000 books with leadership in the title. I do not therefore presume to add to that vast library other than to offer the observations below, having been on both sides of the fence – leading and being led in a number of organisations.

I have worked for few true inspirational leaders, and although in my early working life I would look to senior managers as 'gods', I soon realised that many of them were just like me – a little bewildered by the mechanics and politics of business, but getting by all the same, having found what was required to get on in the world. So what qualities did these individuals have that were admirable or at least useable?

- Most of them had vision. They could paint a picture of a future that you would sign up to. In a war situation if you were in the trenches they would be the ones to lead you over the top. Vision alone is not enough, however. I worked for one director who was tremendous at painting a vision; unfortunately it was a double vision and the director was hopeless at seeing anything through, forever creating a new vision before the old one had had time to became a reality.
- They modelled the behaviours that employees believed to be correct. They acted and behaved in a way that the organisation expected – particularly when new behaviours were being promoted
- They were approachable, they put you at ease, and they were personable. One of the CEOs I worked with had the knack of learning people's names or picking them up from ID cards and the like, and always used your first name – boy did that make you feel important and somehow wanted and valued. He didn't make it seem false and he appeared sincere. I understand that Bill Clinton had this ability of making you feel the most important person in the room.
- They were 'sharp' – quickly picking up the nub of the situation and getting straight to the point. Whether this is a natural ability or something you learn, I am not sure. However, true leaders seem to have this ability in spades.

- They told a good story. This is a characteristic I am particularly interested in, as you will have gathered from previous chapters. I have worked with leaders who have translated their previous experience into stories that were pitched just right for the audience, translated into terms that were relevant to the current company. On the other hand I have worked for 'leaders' whose stories were all about their past experience; they seemed unable to translate the story and the lessons into their current role.

What characteristics have I found to be are important in a leader?

- *Experience*: the ability to translate past experience into stories that are relevant to the current 'team'.
- *Clarity*: the ability to cut through the 'bullshit' and get straight to the crux of the situation.
- *Inspiration*: the ability to provide people with a compelling vision of the future.
- *Environment*: the ability to create a supportive environment and atmosphere which allows people to achieve their full potential.
- *Insight*: the ability to provide insight into the market or company.
- *Honesty*: the ability to engender a belief in their integrity.
- *Humility*: know their own limitations and pick a team who complement their 'shortfalls'.

Many leaders have some of these characteristics but few have them all. I have worked for inspirational leaders who have little insight into what is actually happening in the company; leaders who lead through fear and certainly do not create a supportive environment; leaders who live in the past, as indicated by their inability to translate past experience into current stories, and who continue to tell the same old tales from past companies; and leaders who hide in their office choosing to lead through emails – I am not sure how this last one works really! I remember one leader who I don't think that I ever saw out of his office in the three years I worked for him – that is not literally true but it is how it felt. His staff questioned whether he had legs as they hadn't seen them! He did, but he just didn't feel comfortable out of his 'domain'.

Without good leadership, Innovation within a company or team cannot flourish

Creating the supportive environment is essential to Innovation. Without good leadership Innovation within a company or team cannot flourish – and many Innovation initiatives have failed due to lack of a leader's support. Although it is typically not the leader's direct responsibility to lead any such activities, his/her active involvement will ensure a higher level of success and the stickiness required to gain real value from innovation activities.

Funding

One of the biggest problems facing people with great ideas is getting suitable funding to turn them into a reality whether they be within companies or independent. When starting an organisation the need to have a flexible approach to gaining Innovation funding is vital if you are going to maximise the benefit of any Innovation initiative. As an independent there are many routes, from private financing from friends and relations, through the normal banking route to venture capitalists and business angels. The route taken will be dependent on the scale of investment required. The woman who started the company providing dietary information and menus for diabetics used personal reserves to fund her idea and using this route gained maximum value when the company was sold. This was possible for her because the investment was less than $10,000. Many ideas require more significant funding and therefore different routes need to be explored. Although using these routes will provide access to larger amounts of cash, the downside is that the venture capitalist or other investor will typically require a slice of the action – anything from 20–60 per cent of the company.

Within organisations the story is different and funding is typically provided from either income or capital reserves. Depending on the size and 'sophistication' of the company, the route to funding will vary from organisation to organisation. A typical route would be for individuals to produce a detailed business case which will include estimates of the costs, market size, target audience etc. etc. These business cases can be as short as four pages and as long as 1000.

One of the problems facing would-be innovators within in a company is that most organisations have a long planning cycle – typically three to five years – but only a short budgetary planning cycle, with monies being bid for on an annual basis. This approach allows only those things that are known about at the time of the planning round to be funded; although there is often some 'fat' in the budget, this is usually required for the day-to-day projects that have been underfunded. In some organisations there are 'pots' of money for 'new things'; however these are difficult to access as there is usually no process or methodology for obtaining funds from them, and the money is typically reserved for 'pet' projects in the department or at the director's discretion.

The other issue within large corporates especially is that they want certainty: any money invested must produce a fivefold to tenfold return within a two-year period. Although this is desirable for any project or initiative, it is not realistic when working in the innovation 'space'. In one company I worked with, if an initiative does not make $100 million in five years it is considered a waste of management effort! This company still has the same product set and is starting to drown in the face of competition which does not have the same mindset. Whether it will survive or face the challenge of introducing more flexible funding for new initiatives has yet to be seen but clearly with this approach it cannot survive for long.

Innovation fund

To get round some of these restrictions, companies sometimes look to circumvent the potentially long route to making funding available. In 1997, following a visit to Rank Xerox Parc in California, the director I was working for came back with the idea of an Innovation fund: an internal venture capital fund which would support the Innovative and creative projects that were being thwarted due to lack of available resources. The particular director was a persuasive individual and managed to get his Board colleagues to put aside a million pounds (bear in mind that the company was turning over £6 billion) for an Innovation fund that he would be responsible for. This was effectively bringing an external model of funding for initiatives into the company: if it worked outside in the real world why not within a company?

The Rank Xerox way of managing the fund was not appropriate for our company, as Xerox was primarily a product-based company and I was working for a service-based one. So myself and a couple of colleagues were asked to go away and develop an Innovation fund 'process', a way of giving people access to the available funds whilst ensuring probity and an audit trail for the initiatives. The objective of the fund was to provide an effective way of funding initiatives: to take ideas into reality with as little 'friction' as possible, using a series of checkpoints along the way. What emerged was a four-stage process where any one of the 220,000 people within the company could bid for funding for any idea they had which would have an impact on the bottom line of the company. As the lead director was also the IT director, technology had to feature in the ideas (although in reality only 40–50 per cent of them had a significant technology element).

So a 'fast-track' methodology was developed, supported by four forms which had to be completed – one for each stage of the model – each giving access to further funding:

- Stage 1: Idea development.
- Stage 2: Research.
- Stage 3: Pilot.
- Stage 4: Rollout.

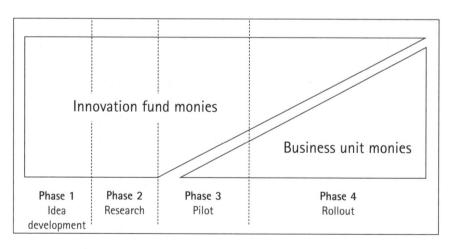

Figure 6 Phases of the Innovation fund process

Stage 1 was the initial seed corn funding of up to £10,000 available to define the concept and to do some preliminary background research.

To illustrate the process, I will use as an example an idea I had to produce dog-repellent trousers for delivery people. I realise this probably will not grip you (as the dog did their legs!) and this idea was a little tongue-in-cheek, but hopefully it will give you a flavour of the way the process worked. The problem of dogs was a serious one at the time (and probably still is), with a number of delivery people getting bitten on a daily basis. The idea was to see if there was a technology solution that could help.

To get access to the funding, the first thing I had to do was to put together a one-page summary which detailed the problem – delivery people being bitten – and my idea for a solution: dog-repellent trousers. This was completed on a pre-printed form available either as a download from the intranet or physically from one of the idea stations around the company.

This initial form had no details of the costs or benefits as they would not be known at this stage, although some idea of scale would be useful: how many delivery people are bitten, how many delivery people wear trousers and what the consequences of their being bitten was. This form was then submitted to the Innovation fund panel, which initially consisted of the technology directors from each of the business units within the company, a total of five plus the main IT director.

The idea was briefly discussed and funding of up to £10,000 was either approved or not. If not, the applicant was given a reason. A problem arose due to the number of people on the panel, who increasingly found it difficult to agree as to what was a suitable idea. Also each of the panel members had his or her own personal agenda, and if an idea didn't fit whatever the member was interested in it didn't get approved. To overcome these issues the panel was subsequently reduced to three people – two of whom were rotated with other business IT managers on a three-monthly basis.

So initial funding had been agreed and the individual who had submitted the idea was given the go-ahead to take the idea forward. This initial funding was to cover further research into the idea. The Innovation fund was administered and supported by the Innovation and Futures team, who had access to a group of 'specialists' in a wide range of fields from vehicles right through to psychology.

The individual would be allocated an Innovation 'angel' who would help him/her get access to the resources required, and to understand fully the problem and the solution. These resources could be either internal to the company – legal advice, delivery people in the case of the dog-repellent trousers, and marketing – or external (typically engaging universities to undertake detailed research, or contacting companies which had products that might be developed to fit the bill).

This initial phase would produce a more detailed report – typically no more than four to six sides of paper – which had further details of the problem: how many delivery people, what were the injuries received, what effect did these injuries have and so on. The report would also detail any ideas for possible solutions, such as fabrics that the trousers could be made of. This latter information would have been obtained through in-house research as well as contacts through universities and company research establishments.

The report would be submitted to the Innovation fund panel and a decision would be taken as to whether the idea was viable and whether further funding – this time up to £25,000 – would be made available. If the decision was yes, a budget code would be issued; if not then an explanation would be provided to the individual who had generated the idea.

If the project was approved then the individual and the Innovation angel would look to take the idea to prototype stage. This is where the project would move forward in earnest, and one of the conditions for further funding was that the individual who had the idea would be given time off for 20 per cent of his/her normal day job to take the idea forward. This was an important factor, as it indicated that the organisation was serious about the idea, and also that the individual who had the idea was the one who drove the idea forward – the one with passion makes the idea a reality.

So, back to our dog-repellent trousers. In this case we would probably have been in contact with a university that had fabric or materials expertise and could already provide some indication as to whether the idea was a possibility. The solution might be a spray that was applied to the trouser material or something in the fabric itself. Let's say for instance that in this case the solution was likely to be a special fabric that had a particular type of thread woven into the material.

The funding would provide funds to get a sample of the material produced and made up into a pair of trousers that could be tested with real dogs. The trousers would be tested in a variety of situations and with a variety of dogs to see if the material was effective and if the trousers were comfortable, or if there were any side effects of the fabric for the wearer.

At the end of this phase the initiating individual and the Innovation angel would prepare a more detailed report for the Innovation fund panel. This would be augmented by relevant people from the organisation who had responsibility for the purchase of uniforms, and the company doctor and representatives from the union and operational management team might get involved. The report back to the panel would be, for the first time, a face-to-face presentation of the project and the results so far. The objective of this session was to persuade the panel that the idea should be take through to a pilot project: rather than a single pair of trousers, a trial of 100 pairs might be suggested.

If funding was agreed, then a small team would be set up, with the initiating individual being released for a short period to join it (as a member or as team leader, depending on the individual). If the decision of the panel were not to go forward, then a written decision would be produced and communicated to all those involved.

Assuming the decision was positive, the dog-repellent trousers trial would be authorised and further funding up to £50,000 would be allocated to the project to take the idea to the next stage. This would involve getting many pairs of trousers made, so a manufacturer would be required along with a panel of volunteer delivery people who would be part of the trial. The trial would go ahead and the results would be monitored in a semi-scientific way – using a control group and the trial group – looking at attacks by dogs and the number of injuries and so on.

The trial would result in a more detailed report, which would look at the feasibility of mass rollout of the trousers, the issues/opportunities of manufacture, an analysis of the durability of the fabric, the trousers' effectiveness and so on. The trial would probably run for three to six months and the funding would provide resources to support the trial – typically university researchers in this case, to undertake the analysis on an ongoing basis.

Again, the results would be presented back to the Innovation fund panel, and if they were successful then rollout of the project would be agreed. Further funding would be expected to come from the business unit that would benefit from the idea at this, the fourth and final stage.

Although the Innovation fund seemed to provide the answer to the problem of supporting ideas and concepts, it fell foul of a number of issues and was shut down in its second year of operation. The most fundamental problem was the concept of tapered funding.

The idea of the fund was that it would provide funding for the first three stages, and if the project looked as though it was going to be successful the business unit that would benefit was expected to find the necessary resources to take the idea into the rollout phase. In the time that the Innovation fund operated, this funding was only available on a very small number of occasions and the Innovation fund itself provided the monies to take ideas into rollout – not the best use of the fund as rollout tended to swallow up large amounts of the cash.

The second problem was that it was very difficult to prove that the fund provided a true bottom-line value to the organisation as the required metrics had never been put in place. The fund had been designed and developed by 'creative' people who had little concept of the need for measurement and governance. When the company focused on the fund 18 months after its launch and measures were retrospectively applied, they highlighted the problems that had gone before and unfortunately this was the beginning of the end.

A further problem was that, as the fund became something that people were interested in, it became a 'process' in its own right and had to have a staff to operate and manage it. The result of bringing in 'operators' was that things slowed down and the ideas 'sifting' became more rigorous – leading to more and more projects not getting through the early stages.

This approach caused people to lose faith in the initiative, and the pool of new ideas began to dry up. This left the Innovation fund team with a small number of ideas that were 'forced' through to the latter stages, and although these may not have been suitable for rollout they were taken through to that stage because there was nothing else to work on. The result was that at the end of the fund's life there were just three projects, and they were cycling through the pilot/rollout phases over and over. The pilot would produce inconclusive results but they would try to roll it out, and then when it failed they would try to pilot a new approach to the same issue – missing out the idea generation and research phases completely, just cycling through the last two phases, trying to find a way of making something work that didn't have a chance.

The last problem was that the business saw the fund as a 'slush fund' for product and service development – a way of funding the normal day-to-day stuff that hadn't been budgeted for or had been underfunded. As I mentioned earlier the long budget-planning cycle meant that very often there were shortfalls in the day-to-day funding of activities and initiatives. Weak management at the time allowed this to happen, and it not only devalued the fund but also sent the wrong message out to the company as a whole.

The Innovation fund provided the seed-corn funding for over 160 projects, of which around 25 were taken through into the later phases and rolled out. How many of these actually delivered the benefits that were originally predicted is not known and I guess, because the necessary governance and measurement procedures where not put in place, they never will be known. The fund closed two years after it started. It had consumed a couple of million pounds and had certainly fostered and encouraged an Innovative atmosphere. Did it affect the bottom line? Anecdotally, it generated £600m of new business and benefit.

Could this be proved? Well no, not really, as it was never tracked. Very often, although initial funding had come from the fund, when income was generated it was never associated with the fund – it was always 'owned' by the business unit. In retrospect a more rigorous management framework should be put in place and the fund should be run as a profit centre in its own right. Any initiative that was funded would be tracked and a percentage of the benefit or income would be paid back into the fund, which would provide funding for the next initiative.

As an aside, the dog-repellent idea never got through the first phase as it was thought too 'way-out'. However, I still think there is something in it and delivery people are still getting bitten on a regular basis – maybe I'll …

So what did we learn from the Innovation fund initiative? Chiefly,

we learned about what was needed to make such an initiative successful. To some degree this mirrors the 10-step approach discussed
throughout this book; however there is a clear subset of factors which
are more important in the context of an Innovation fund.

- First is the need for a good champion at a senior level within the
  organisation – someone who sees the value and is prepared to
  fight for it. Without this it is highly unlikely to have the success it
  needs to survive.
- Second is access to a pool of resources – money, people and ideas.
  Clearly the financial side of the equation is important, but funding alone is not a guarantee of success; huge amounts of money
  can lead to complacency, as happened in our case. If there are few
  financial constraints, people become lazy and don't try to truly
  Innovate. They go for the more traditional, more conservative
  ideas which are easy to implement.
- The third, and maybe the most important, factor in the long-
  term success of any such initiative is a way of measuring the
  success or otherwise of the fund. If there is no proper system to
  measure performance, then when the initiative comes under the
  spotlight it is too easy for the fund to be curtailed or even
  cancelled, as it is considered a 'waste of money'.
- Fourth, there must be access to good people to generate the ideas
  or to help them come to fruition. Let's first look at the support
  staff who will help the people generating the ideas to turn them
  into a reality. In my experience, the more eclectic the team of
  advisors the better, as this injects a level of serendipity to the
  equation by bringing new views, ideas and linkages to the
  'process'. In terms of the ideas themselves, there are several ways
  of stimulating, generating and gathering them, and this is
  discussed in some detail elsewhere in this book. The most
  successful ideas, in my experience, come from the people doing
  the job (the workforce) or receiving the particular product or
  service (the customers).
- Fifth, the success or failure of any Innovation fund initiative will
  depend on active communication – telling people how good it is and
  how it is benefiting the organisation. In the 10-step approach this is
  called the 'dance of Innovation' (covered in detail in Step 5). In the

context of the Innovation fund however, the emphasis should be placed on gaining positive external communication rather than on internal communication. The benefit of this is that external 'plaudits' will ensure continued support at senior level – which as discussed previously will at least ensure continued funding and thereby the continuity of the fund itself.

- Lastly the fund should be self funding after the first year. In other words, any funded initiative should put back into the fund a percentage of any income or benefit realised. This last point would focus activity around the fund and make people think hard before bidding for monies, as they would have to declare the results of their work and be accountable for the outcome. It should be recognised however that not all projects will provide a tangible benefit. A success rate of somewhere between 10 and 15 per cent should be aimed for – any more and you will stifle those wacky ideas that may make you a million!

External funding

One of the options for companies and individuals is to gain external funding through venture capitalists or corporate venture specialists. Larger companies tend not to favour this option, as they usually lose some of the equity in the idea or project. It is vital for both parties to really understand the 'deal' and the drivers before entering into this type of relationship. Many companies fail to do this and end up in a situation where the contract is not suitable or in the worst case actually harmful to one or both parties – usually the corporate party involved.

Venture capital

Most venture capitalists prefer to invest in 'entrepreneurial businesses'. This does not necessarily mean they are only interested in small or new businesses; rather, it has to do with the potential for growth, the company's or individual's aspirations. These businesses or individuals are aiming to grow rapidly to a significant size in a reasonably short space of time. As a rule of thumb, unless a business can offer the prospect of significant turnover growth within five years, it is unlikely to be of interest to any venture capital firm. This type of investor is typically only interested in companies with good high-growth prospects, managed by experienced and ambitious teams who are capable of turning their business plans into reality.

Corporate venturing

The term 'corporate venturing' covers a range of mutually beneficial relationships between companies. The relationships range from those between companies within the same group, through those between unrelated companies, to collective investment by companies in other companies through a fund. The companies involved may be of any size, but such relationships are commonly formed between a larger company and a smaller independent one, usually in a related line of business.

The larger company may invest in the smaller company, and so provide an alternative or supplementary source of finance. It may, instead or also, make available particular skills or knowledge, perhaps in technical or management areas, which a smaller company would otherwise not have access to. Another possible benefit is to provide access to established marketing and distribution channels, or complementary technologies.

I have had direct experience of putting together such corporate venturing deals. It is an interesting experience, although the companies involved did lose quite a bit of income, credibility and sometimes brand value by moving down this road. In most cases the projects do get off the ground as both parties are keen to make the relationship happen – there is very often a 'honeymoon' period where the relationship is great. However, problems very often start to occur when delivery of whatever it is starts or there are problems with the product or service. Very often in the adrenaline rush of start-up, failure is never planned for and this leads to contractual problems further down the road. This is why fully understanding the reasons for getting into a relationship, along with the expectations and drivers, is vital for both parties, and so is an exit strategy. My maxim in these relationship is to 'plan for the worst and hope for the best'.

* * *

The environmental factors and resources have been discussed in some detail in Step 3. All the factors discussed provide some level of positive effect on any initiative; in reality however, the way they are furnished depends on the level of resources available.

All the factors discussed can be found for free – well, almost – if sought creatively, and there doesn't need to be huge investment. In fact I am sure that there is some inverse correlation: the larger the investment and the more people involved, the smaller the benefit. So be inventive and creative in creating your environment for change.

On a personal note again, these factors are all relevant for you as an individual – you can find creative places all around you if you just look. They are typically places where you have little to distract you, or if there is distraction it is 'natural'. For me it is the bathroom or while driving or, as I do a lot of trekking, out in the middle of nowhere. I know people who get their best thoughts over a coffee at Starbucks or whilst listening to rock music (a recent study in the USA suggests that a noisy environment actually helps the thought process). In the end it is really what works for you – find out and then *just do it*!

Chapter 5

Step 4. The barriers to Innovation

Any major activity within a company is going to come up against barriers: things that are going to stop it happening. Some of these will be predictable, some will be evident and some not. The idea of this fourth step is to try and flush out what these barriers might be and to look for potential solutions early on in any activity – rather than waiting for them to hit you when it's too late to do anything about them. This tactical approach is one that I have seen over and over in many large projects, not just innovation initiatives but projects in general.

For many people – particularly those optimists and those of us who think incrementally – these barriers tend to be surprises: things that we never thought would happen but of course always will when not foreseen. For some people solving these problems is what they live for, so not planning for them can be a positive thing: fire fighting in some organisations is rewarded! This is something that always used to irk me as people who hadn't planned properly – those who 'had' to work weekends because something had gone wrong – were given recognition awards, while those who planned for everything and whose projects went smoothly were never recognised. This approach, which is seen in a number of organisations, encourages people to not plan, not think the unthinkable and adopt a laid-back approach to risk management and planning.

Innovation initiatives are special. You may think I am bound to say that, but when looking at what will stop them becoming a reality you have to treat them as such. The normal processes and procedures for 'barrier management' that operate within organisations are typically focussed on normal day-to-day operations and not to the discontinuous initiatives that come out of any innovation activity.

The traditional approach to identifying barriers and risks is to ask the sponsors what they think the barriers will be. Although this approach is viable however, it may not flush out the real issues. A second approach would be to get a small team or a focus group together and run a workshop to find out what they thought the barriers would be. Again this is valid but may give a restricted view. I have tried both, and in my early days of trying to get Innovative activities going I thought that this would be enough. However I learned that to really understand what the issues and barriers might be, the more people you get involved the better – hence our approach of undertaking a questionnaire among over 200 senior managers in a national UK organisation.

The survey has already been discussed in Chapter 3. As we saw there, the six 'things' that this group felt were stopping change – stopping new ideas coming to fruition and discouraging people from taking their ideas forward – were:

- Culture   '... we don't do things like that.'
- History   '... that's not the sort of thing we would get involved in.'
- Permission '... it isn't my job.'
- Space   '... the environment just isn't conducive to thinking.'
- Time   '... I just don't have time to think.'
- Money   '... I don't have any spare money in my budget for new things.'

In this chapter we will explore each of these in some detail as well as looking at areas identified by other organisations and individuals. In a survey of 1000 people within an organisation, 42 per cent felt that culture was the main barrier to innovation and 27 per cent felt history was the main problem. Actually less than 8 per cent felt that money was the issue although nearly everybody put it in their top three barriers. People ranked permission, space and time in equal proportions, with on average 12 per cent of people citing them in their top three barriers.

Culture

As previously mentioned, culture is an intangible thing that appears to be transmitted around the organisation via stories. These stories are seldom narrated as such, but told as an interpretation of company behaviour and passed down from individual to individual. The danger of this is that on every re-telling individuals interpret the 'culture', emphasising certain aspects of it and de-emphasising others.

This approach has been used for millennia within societies where storytelling is a way of perpetuating societal norms: North American Indians, the Chinese, Aborigines, and some Asian and island cultures. These societies have almost formalised the stories, and although they are rarely written down they are sometimes represented pictorially. Stories are highly important to these societies and the people who know and tell them are usually held in high esteem.

The stories comprise and perpetuate the culture of these societies and are told with great attention to detail. They usually transmit lessons and values that the society holds dear.

There are a number of consultancy companies that are taking the concept of these societal stories and are using them within companies, usually to communicate particular strategies or approaches – sometimes bringing in individuals from the storytelling societies, particularly the North American Indians, to help the process. Although there is evidence of culture change taking place as a result of these stories, I have found no evidence of an active programme of using stories to actually change the culture of the company, to use them in an active manner to 'steer' the culture in a particular direction.

The idea of *strategic storytelling* was developed in the Innovation Lab environment to research the concept of using stories and storytelling to affect corporate culture. I had attended a meeting with the chairman of a large multinational company, who interspersed the session with a liberal smattering of stories and anecdotes. I recognised that there was something happening here. Something was different about this person: he was connecting with the audience in a way that was somehow exciting. His use of stories made what he was saying 'come alive' for the people involved. The audience appeared to be 'actively' listening to what was being said rather than letting the presentation wash over them as so many times happens.

	Yesterday	Today	Tomorrow
Non-fiction	Case study	Meeting	Plan
Enhanced reality		News	Strategic storytelling
Fiction	Legends		Scenario

Figure 7 Stories

I spoke to as many of the audience as I could afterwards to see if I was the only one who had felt that there was something happening in that room, and most people had 'connected' with the guy. A few people commented that they could see themselves in the situations he had painted and felt empathy with him, understanding how he felt (many of the comments had an emotional flavour – clearly the guy had engaged people at an emotional level: he was *making it real* for people). Interestingly I met a few of the people who had been at the session a few months later at another conference and I was surprised that they remembered the session and could relate the stories he told almost word for word – they also said that they had used his stories in their own work situations to illustrate some point or other. Clearly something special had happened in the room that day – so I decided to pursue this further.

Following on from this I got involved in the whole area of stories and how they could be actively used within business. I read the books that had been published and was slightly disappointed that most of them were using stories to tell the history of the company, not to influence the future. So a technique was developed for use within the Innovation Lab environment: teams would develop 'future stories' as part of the workshops – visualise them either as a rich picture or montage of images. They might perform them as a story or fairy tale, or as a series of conversations, or simply write them down.

Each of these methods reinforces and clarifies the key messages and helps the group articulate their particular vision or strategy. The essence of the story is then disseminated though all available channels to the rest of the organisation, team or affected group.

One of the consultants working in the area of storytelling told me a couple of things about stories that I have never forgotten. Firstly he said that whenever people listen to a presentation or read a book or whatever, they do it in two modes. In the first, they are paying attention to what is being said or read. But there is a second mode that is then putting them in the particular situation being discussed, translating whatever is being presented into their own particular situation: 'How is this going to affect me?' 'How would I respond/react in this situation?' The use of stories provides a short cut for the second mode by doing the translation for you – speeding up your ability to understand how something may affect you or your situation. The second thing he told me was that stories have persistence – and I decided to put this to the test. Whilst facilitating workshops I would split the group and get them to feed back whatever it was they were working on in a number of different ways. First as a story – sometimes as a '*strategic fairy tale*' – second as a PowerPoint presentation, third as a conversation, where two people are discussing the solution or whatever it was, and finally as a report or document.

What is fascinating is that each type of feedback has a particular persistence when people in the session are questioned at periods afterwards. The stories have the greatest persistence, with people able to remember the essence if not the words up to two months later, whereas a PowerPoint presentation lasts typically for less than a week (usually three days!). Pictures and conversations sit somewhere in between the two. This research seems to prove the power of stories and their potential impact on the culture of the company.

One reason stories are a particularly powerful way of connecting with people is that they make it easy for people to interpret what is being said. Some of the best presenters use stories in their orations, allowing people to quickly understand the point in question, allowing them to understand how whatever it is will or could impact them. My own view is that some of the best leaders are the ones that use anecdotes of their experiences to reinforce and clarify their point and message – and some of the worst leaders are the ones that haven't updated/interpreted their stories for the current situation.

I worked for one director who was still telling the same old story of a company he had worked at over five years ago. Although he might have thought it applicable, people found it really hard to understand how it was relevant to them and their situation. He had not bothered, or maybe had not been able, to update the story to the current situation by transferring the moral and lessons to his new audience. Rather than the anecdote or story helping the situation, it was actually confusing it – making it more difficult rather than easier. He was telling a story that the audience couldn't identify with, that was about a completely different industry and country! I watched the people round the table when he was telling the story yet again, and their faces told their own story. I guess the guy lost a lot of personal credibility that day. The frustrating thing was that if you unpicked the essence of the tale it was relevant: there was a good moral and lessons that could be applicable. He just didn't understand the concept of storytelling – particularly standing in 'other people's shoes'! I think he was telling the story for himself rather than his audience – I heard recently that he is still telling the same stories some three years on.

History

There is little that can be done about the history of the company, although companies can minimise its impact on Innovation by highlighting some of the more interesting aspects of their past. There is evidence that new start-up companies – which have little history – are better placed than those companies that have a long and traditional one.

It is interesting that where countries have lost much of their documented history, customs and traditions through conflict, war or natural disaster, they have often rebuilt themselves and have in some cases re-written their history. Some of these countries are now leading the world in commerce and business.

The fact that the UK has over a thousand years of documented history has, in my opinion, stopped it moving forward, because a country's culture and social traditions set the norms by which society acts. The changes in many countries' demographics, with increased migration and the development of new cultural communities – sometimes bounded within particular areas of a city – have and are changing their cultures. New stories are being communicated which will, by definition, change society – most likely within a generation.

So how can you minimise the historical baggage that companies carry? The first thing is to recognise that it's there. It needs to be recognised that the company has a history and it must be understood, particularly what aspects are affecting current business practices and culture. Many organisations – particularly those that were born out of monopoly or government ownership – had much of their history written down in manuals that were the guidebooks for the way things were done. Some organisations have carried this concept into the modern age by transferring them onto the intranet. These 'instruction manuals' are generally guarded carefully, and typically have people who are responsible for their upkeep and maintenance. It is not only the manuals themselves that can be detrimental to doing things differently: the mere requirement to write everything down can be disempowering for organisations.

I was working recently with a large UK company undertaking some product development work, and as normal I had designed a new product development framework for them. This consisted of a fast-track approach that would get new products to market within 90 days – an unheard of result for this particular organisation and one which they were rightly proud of. I went back into the organisation four months after my contract, and asked how the fast-track process was going. I was shown what they had turned it into: facing me were 16 manuals on how to implement what had now become a very 'slow-track' process. My 90 days had turned into a 200-day process and nothing was being delivered. They, had spent their time shadowing an initiative and writing it all down. They were very proud of the manuals and the flowcharts and everything but they had lost the plot on what they were trying to achieve. This approach holds the company back however, as the formalisation of the task actually stops any changes to the way things are done, in order to maintain a stable company and to stop any disruptive activity – Innovation.

Permission

This is actually one of the easiest barriers to explain. It is easy to sort out in the short term but very difficult to deal with long term. In workshops and meetings people are 'allowed' to be different or do things in new ways, which is a very liberating experience. I have worked in many workshops where people are hugely excited about the process or output – they have come out with some fantastic ideas which could revolutionise the company or the way that it works. I have recently been undertaking a series of workshops with a large UK government department using the Jack Welsh Workout methodology/process. The workshops take junior frontline staff and encourage them to generate ideas about the work they do – how they can improve things in their own work area and take out the unnecessary tasks and activities that add no value to the work. When asked why they hadn't made these improvements already, the answer is: 'Nobody gave me permission to.' Had they ever asked? Who did they expect to give them permission? Why should somebody think to give them permission? What is permission anyway – if the idea is good why would anybody stop you?

The excitement this type of activity generates is incredible. People get so excited about the ideas they have and usually the commitment on the day is superb. Yet the evidence from numerous workshops is that only 30 per cent of the ideas generated on these workshops – even though they are great ideas and there is a solid business case for making them happen – actually make it from an idea into action. So what stops people – other than natural cynicism? When asked, a typical answer is 'I didn't think I had permission to do ...' The perception had changed from 'Nobody gave me' to 'I didn't think I had'. Even though a senior member of the team had given them the 'right' to make whatever it was happen, there was/is a self-limiting belief, some internal belief, value or learned behaviour, that somehow they don't have this mythical 'permission'.

Unfortunately, in the longer term (i.e. when people get back to their normal job), they quickly spring back to the company norm, which typically disempowers individuals. Very often this lack of activity is due to the sheer pressure of work or seemingly urgent tasks that take priority over changes that are probably more important to the company than anything else.

For myself I have never really asked for permission, and have always said to my team that it is easier to ask for forgiveness than for permission. This to me speaks to the Nike slogan – Just Do It! In my 12 years of working in Innovation and employing this maxim, I have only had to ask for forgiveness twice and have certainly done many radical things. If I had asked for permission to do many of them it would certainly not have been given, and in a number of cases I would probably have been dismissed.

I have found that many managers just do not have the vision to see past the current situation and 'don't know what they don't know'. Once whatever has been implemented or done, they couldn't do without whatever it was. An example of this is the Innovation Lab. At the time, although I didn't know what I was doing, I had a vision of what I thought the company needed and a clear idea of what I wanted to do. If we had had to put together a business case and prove the net present value (NPV) and all the other financial controls, we would never have created the facility. If we had asked permission to create something that resembled a theme park, I am sure that we would have been refused point blank. However, because we just got on with it and made it happen, we achieved the impossible. Once we had built the facility the company could not do without it – the other interesting factor was that once it was successful it was everybody's idea, but that to me is a sign of success.

Space

Physical space is something we all need – and typically the more the better. However as the population increases and the pressures for efficiencies are increased, then our ability to have the luxury of space disappears. When we did our survey, people complained about their lives being too cluttered, both at work and at home. Many companies have a clear-desk policy, along with a governance procedure to ensure that this is adhered to. What many people do is either ignore it or sweep their papers into a drawer at the end of the day – resulting in lost files, papers and other important documents. Interestingly for me this approach also is relevant to the computer: nobody archives, and files are scattered all over the place – some in folders some not – and the result is that nothing can be found.

The offices and building we work in are also not usually conducive to Innovation – or even normal thinking! We have little or no chance to tailor our offices, and with the advent of air conditioning we cannot even get fresh air into our lives. I was working in the USA recently and was amazed that Dilbert is real: the cubicle world really does exist. Coming from the UK where personal offices are very much a thing of the past and open-plan is the norm even for senior management, the world of cubicles is unreal. The cubicle creates an insular mentality where people don't seem to communicate: the first two weeks I was there I spent my time encouraging people to talk to each other – to share knowledge and experience.

So in your work environment think about the space you need around you to work effectively, and then think about how you can achieve it.

Time

I have discussed at some length the concept of the Innovation space, the physical thinking environment, so I won't go through it again. The other aspect of space relates to having time in the daily grind to think. As many companies are facing changes in their external environments which are placing increasing pressures on them to rationalise, cut costs and so on, they are placing increasing pressures on the staff that are left – expecting them to do more, increasing their responsibility (of course without the accountability) and demanding longer hours. This environment of change brings high levels of uncertainty for these staff, typically middle or senior managers. An outcome of this is their need to be visible, usually through attendance at an increasing number of meetings. I have seen examples of senior managers who are in constant meetings from 08:30 in the morning through to 7 pm; they also have to handle emails, post and phone calls and to read seemingly endless papers and briefing notes as well – and then there is the Blackberry which allows you to work when you are not at work! There is definitely no space in these people's working lives to have *any* ideas never mind innovative ones!

So how can we create space/time to allow ideas to emerge? Well, some of the great leaders of our time have conscientiously taken time just to think – or not as the case may be. The concept of not-thinking is alien to most of us. I certainly find it very difficult. However clearing one's mind is one of the best ways of letting great ideas come to you. Meditation is one technique that can be used, but many people also find that sport or creative arts are just as powerful. Many leaders have used solitude as a technique. One of the most famous recently was Margaret Thatcher, who apparently would just go and sit quietly and not think of anything – letting go of the day-to-day strains and thoughts and letting the 85 per cent of the mind that we don't normally use take over.

This technique is taught by a number of 'management gurus' and is very powerful. However in an activity-based/meeting management environment it is hard to justify – although the benefits can be huge.

The concept of a management retreat was all the rage some years ago as were Outward Bound and other such events. Although they were targeted at team building and team trust, these also had the effect of giving people 'space' to be, to clear their mind. On some of these types of events I have found some great inspiration for day-to-day problems back at the office.

If you can't take work out then take time out

I would encourage the concept of 'time out' where rather than take unnecessary work out of your job or role, you look for opportunities to take time out instead. This can be very difficult as if you are not careful you, or your secretary/assistant/team, will fill it up with more meetings and other tasks. The benefits of an hour of doing nothing each day will pay off ten-fold in your effectiveness.

We all complain about not having enough time, and for some this may be true. It is more likely, however, that we do not allocate the time we have appropriately – letting other people and pressure dictate how we spend the little time we have. I know of managers who attend six meetings per day, respond to 150 emails and have to read several reports, as well as answering their phones and of course actually doing what they are being paid to do.

So how can you give yourself more time? Well, apart from the impossibility of being a time lord there are some strategies that should help with your days. I have read and tried most of the accepted thinking on management, from one-minute manager, though moving cheeses to *The Tao of Pooh* and beyond. Indeed it was one such course that changed my life back in 1989 when I picked up Brian Tracey's Psychology of Achievement tapes.

I have developed an approach based loosely on the Workout principles from GE, but instead of taking work out of people's jobs, in my approach you are giving them time out – giving them time back to do things that are important to them and their jobs. OK, so nothing radical there I hear you say.

I first ask people to keep a rough log of their activities during the day for a couple of weeks. No detail, yet, of the day structure itself but just a list on a day-by-day basis of the sort of things they have been doing. I then ask them to annotate this list, using three categories: things they *have* to do, things they *need* to do and things they *want* to do.

- *Things you have to do*: These are things that you have to do as part of your life or your job. In a career sense they will be in your job description, and in your home life they will be things that you need to do to survive – pay bills, shop, cook food and so on. (Some of you may pay other people to do these things, but that is a luxury not many people can afford.) The things you have to do could link to the business plan or the financial goals of the business or your life plan if you have one.
- *Things you need to do*: I use need in this context for things that are demanded of you by other people – using guilt, pity or power or whatever other techniques they use to 'control' you. These are the things that are delegated from above or passed up from below but will require time and effort on your part. Typically you have no control over these things and usually they are extremely time consuming.
- *Things you want to do*: These are things that you really want to do – things that could be new or off the wall or personal-growth oriented. The things that we all say 'I wish I could find time to …' We all have these in our mind but due to other pressures never

seem to get round to getting them done. At some stage in our lives we will be too old or infirm to do these, and will regret it.

So we have our list of activities for the days we have recorded, and each activity should annotated with an H, N or W for Have, Need and Want. When I did this exercise to try out my theory, I was amazed that 70 per cent of what I was doing on a daily basis was in the need category, 28 per cent of it was have and less than 2 per cent was in the want category.

The aim was is to rebalance this so that you get to do more of what you *want* to do (60 per cent) and less of what you *need* to do (less than 10 per cent) and the right amount of what you *have* to do (30 per cent). So how do you get this re-balance?

I reviewed a week's worth of the *needs* category elements and plotted them on a simple mind-map that placed the *needs* category items on it according to where the need had arisen. Using this methodology you can see where your potential problems lie. If all the *needs* come from your boss, then you should be trying to convert those into *have*'s – things that are in your objectives or job description; if they are coming from your staff, then you should revisit their objectives or consider whether they need personal development to enhance their skills.

An alternative way is to review your *need* activities if they are all arising from projects and initiatives. Look at what you would have done differently on these projects had you known what you know now – what was the root cause? Although some of this is typically picked up in a post-implementation review or project review, these will not look at the situation from a personal perspective – only from a project one. So the company might not make the mistake again but the need will still be placed on you on other projects and work situations.

As an aside, I had a mission (which interestingly I failed on) in my last company to have an email-free day – one day where you would not be allowed to use email but had to talk to people again. In a US study by one of the leading consultancies, it was reported that more than 70 per cent of internal emails went less than 10 metres. What happened to picking up the phone or talking?

I look around offices today at lunchtime and I see nearly all the staff sat at their desks eating sandwiches or some hot noodle dish.

What happened to the lunch break? That was an ideal time to take time out to think, to refresh yourself and recharge your batteries. In the rush to get more out of people the lunch break has gone – people are using the time to catch up on the dreaded email. What is also bad about this is that eating at your desk can actually harm your health. Studies in the US and UK found that there were more germs and bacteria on your computer keyboard and cell phone than there were in the toilet!

Money

This is one of the easiest as well as one of the hardest issues for investment in Innovative and speculative areas. That sounds confusing and so it is. The issue of investment needs to be considered carefully as it will probably be the single factor that will either bring life or death to any initiative.

One of the issues I have faced over my time in Innovation is the cyclical nature of the investment that companies seem to make in these sometimes intangible areas. Investment is made at the start of the initiative – whether this is an Innovation activity or some strategic goal – and then after a period typically of around 14–18 months funding is reviewed and often cut back. In the company I worked in, they had around a three and a half year cycle of investment, which was reflected in staffing and funding. The graph below, which is taken from actual figures, demonstrates this cycle clearly. From it you can see that the staffing level peaked at just over 20 people, and investment at £2.2m for new initiatives.

The company realises that it needs to do something different, so it invests in Innovation or some other similar initiative which drives the Innovation investment model. As the company doesn't know what it expects or what the model can do, it is disappointed with the results, so when the following year's budget is laid down the funding is cut. This cycle is repeated a couple of times until there is no funding and all the individuals previously involved have either left the company or moved into more 'normal' line management roles. At this stage the company realises it needs to invest in Innovation, or some other similar initiative, and the cycle starts again.

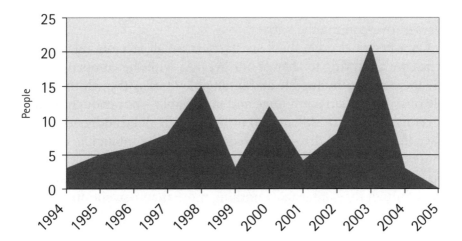

Figure 8 Cycles of investment

Various companies have similar initiatives. I have recognised similar cycles of investment – periods of plenty and famine, in other organisations. Very often the cycles are slightly different – some longer and some slightly shorter –and there does not appear to be a correlation between the cycles and the industry or market segment. So one of the questions is: How can you smooth the investment?

The first thing is to do Steps 1, 2 and 3 of this book: understand what you are trying to achieve, understand where you are now, and understand what is stopping you getting to where you want to go. It is important to put in place realistic and appropriate measures so that the value of any Innovation initiative is realised and acknowledged by those who matter within the company – typically the CEO and the finance director.

* * *

In this step we looked at what was going to stop Innovation happening and how this could be outflanked or avoided. The barriers seem to be reasonably standard in the companies I have worked with, and as I have discussed are split between the tangible and the intangible. The tangibles tend to be easy to fix, while the intangibles need some 'creativity' to identify what the real problem is and come up with ways of overcoming the barrier.

On a personal note, there are barriers we all face on a daily basis when we are trying to change our lives. As with the company example there are both tangible and intangible ones. Although the tangible ones very often seem huge and unsolvable – not enough money, no contacts, lack of skill and so on – they can all be addressed if you have the focus and drive to overcome them. The intangible ones are more difficult as they tend to be the self-limiting beliefs that we have built up over our lives – things that we convince ourselves are true, even though they are usually nothing more than perception.

Chapter 6

Step 5. The dance of Innovation

I have already discussed the need to communicate success and failure in the area of Innovation and to give people 'permission' to think, act and perform differently. This chapter covers the topic of the communication that is required to help make this a reality.

When researching for the book, I got to thinking of the parallels between the bee model discussed in Step 1 and the whole Innovation activity within companies. One of the things the bees do when they find a new food source is come back to the hive and dance in such a way that they communicate the direction and distance of the new food source. Now I am not suggesting that we start a new dance craze by getting teams to devise a new dance that communicates their great idea, the size and shape of the market and so on (though maybe this isn't such a crazy idea after all!). However the concept of telling other people in the organisation in such a way that they want to follow and find the new 'food source' is very powerful.

The method of communication – as with the bees – is very important to the effectiveness of the message transmitted. In many organisations communication is left to team meetings, the intranet or the internal newspaper/journal. In the right company and situation the internal journal is powerful in its own right, but I have found that the impact and effectiveness of this format can be restrictive as you lose the passion and personal nature of the message.

One of the most effective enablers for Innovation happened way back in the early 1990s at the peak of the total quality management boom. The company I worked for at the time held an annual fair for all the total quality management initiatives that were happening in the company. Initiatives had to compete for a place at the fair and each one then had a booth where its staff set up their stall. Over a two-week period nearly everyone in the company visited the fair and saw the 60-plus stands, where the people involved in the initiatives told their story – over and over. At the time, I don't think people realised what they were doing as the fair was focussed very much on incremental improvements in the day-to-day operation of the business.

One of the impacts of this approach was to get best practice out across the company, as people would pick up ideas from these stands and then go back and implement them locally. They had a contact who they could phone up and ask questions and they felt empowered to do something: 'If they are doing this, then it must be OK for me to do it too'.

The second effect of this fair was the culture change that rippled through the company. New stories were being told by the people who had the passion and vision for whatever it was they had achieved – sometimes something very small, at other times major company changes. Many of the ideas were very simple but had a huge potential impact on the company in efficiency terms and in some cases financial benefits to the bottom line.

The atmosphere at the fair was electric – the sheer presence of so many positive people in one space was almost overpowering. The interaction and sometimes competition between the different stalls created intense excitement so that just being in there was very special. People came away with a real 'can-do' attitude. I am not sure how long that lasted, but it certainly caused a stir in the company.

Running such an event today would be almost impossible as the cost to the company in both lost revenue and the cost of the fair would be prohibitive. However the concept can be brought up to date through the use of the Internet – an online version of the ideas fair. But rather than use two-dimensional pages of text and pictures, use the medium of video to communicate the passion and vision. The advent of video-podcasting, either to personal MP3/video players or PC/MAC screens, could be the saviour of culture change within organisations, as is has both low costs and very high impact.

This step of the process is so important to making the Innovation culture sticky that it warrants further exploration. When you talk to individuals, as I have done, from a wide range of companies the same words keep coming back to me: 'Its not my job to have ideas,' 'We have a department somewhere that does that,' 'I just get on with what I am told to do' and many other such phrases. People feel that they don't have permission to think or do things differently. This concept of permission is one that I think is key to creating a groundswell in the organisation – and ultimately making Innovation and change sticky.

As I mentioned earlier in the book, I have been working with a large organisation on a programme using the Workout methodology from GE, which encourages frontline staff to 'take work out' of their daily jobs, eliminate the things that don't add value to the company or the activity. What has been fascinating has been the feeling of helplessness the individuals involved have about the way things are done and their inability to change what very often are ineffective, pointless and repetitive tasks. Although some great ideas have come out of the workshops, the real benefit has come out of the people going back into the organisation and giving their colleagues permission to start thinking about changing the way they work.

The individuals are embarking on the 'dance of Innovation' without knowing it. They are emulating the bees – going back into the organisation and giving people permission to be, think and act differently. In this particular programme this is not something that is being done consciously and it is not seen as a particularly important factor, though it is key to the culture change the activity is targeted at. The benefits are being measured around the amount of hours saved and not the change in the culture that is happening in the background – you are what you measure! Although this is a programme focussed on incremental change, the same effect can be seen for the more radical Innovative changes.

So how do you actively promote the 'dance of Innovation'? Well the first thing is to actually recognise the dance as an important factor as well as recognising the changes in the culture that are taking place as a result of the activity. As mentioned in Step 2 earlier in the book, it is recommended that you should assess the current state of the culture so that any changes can be measured and recorded. If this activity is undertaken it is important that the characteristics you are trying to change or influence are actively measured and monitored.

This can be done through a number of activities, depending on the factors that are being considered. If the culture change is targeted at improving customer service, then surveys of the customers are a possible method, while if the activity is focussed on changing staff behaviour, then staff surveys should be used.

Reinforcing the message and activities through other media such as internal newsletters, notice boards and the intranet as well as external press and magazine articles can enhance the impact of the 'dance of Innovation'. (One observation here is that one external press or magazine article is worth 10–15 internal articles as it provides the all-important industry recognition and therefore garners senior management support). All these activities not only have the benefit of informing people of what is going on and the benefits that are being realised, but more importantly they give people permission to do things themselves – telling people it is OK to try something new.

The impact of this permission is to encourage new activities, new ideas, new ways of working and behaviour. It is important that the support structure is in place to provide whatever people need to turn their ideas into a reality. The lack of such resources can not only have a very negative effect on the subsequent culture change but can also suppress the initial programme – in my case the GE Workout initiative.

It is vital, therefore, to support the dance of Innovation (or whatever you like to call it) if maximum benefit is to be obtained from any initiative. The need for this support should be recognised and it must be planned for before the initiative is started. How this is undertaken is dependent on the company involved and the objectives of the initiative. There are a number of mechanisms that can be used however, and these are detailed below:

- *Intrigue*: Prior to starting any such initiative, one very positive activity that I have found works extremely well is an intrigue campaign where the initiative is 'trailed' to raise awareness and to get people talking about whatever it is. This technique is used very successfully in the movie business and, as discussed earlier, much can be learned from looking at examples in other industries and either emulating or adopting them.
- *Open days/surgeries*: The need to de-mystify the initiatives/ activities can be an issue – particularly where the company has a

decentralised or highly dispersed workforce. By making it 'easy' to find out what is happening you will encourage people to get involved – particularly when the 'engagement' is done on a personal level – i.e. on a one-to-one basis. Many companies try to do this via the intranet or via email, but although these are both acceptable forms of communication they lack the personal element. Also, the messages can get lost in the myriad of other emails and other communications, particularly in organisations where managers and staff are bombarded with endless messages.

- *Articles*: As mentioned previously, external media articles – particularly in a national or global magazine, for example a case study in the *Harvard Business Review* or an article in the *Economist* – can have a huge impact on the internal credibility of the initiative. In my own case, when we first launched the Innovation Lab we had an article in the *Financial Times*, a mainstream UK broadsheet newspaper, as well as a short mention on a major UK popular science programme on the BBC, *Tomorrows World*. The impact of just these two, admittedly significant, pieces of journalism was out of all proportion to the 'investment' in them. Suddenly we had more visitors than we could cope with, more visits from senior management than we had ever had before, and a commitment to continued funding.

- *Internal communications*: The benefit and impact of formal internal communications can be a little haphazard. If it is done well the communication can have a tremendous effect on the organisation; if done badly (which a high proportion seem to be), it may have disastrous effects! So how can you ensure you do the former rather than the latter?

* * *

The 'dance' is something we all do on a daily basis in our own right: we are all passionate about something – or someone. We communicate most effectively when we are passionate about an issue and this is what I mean by the 'dance'. In a corporate situation is very rare to find anyone who is passionate about anything other than whatever they do outside work! The key is to transfer some of that passion into initiatives and activities that lead to whatever the vision is. The other factor is that enthusiasm and passion are infectious – they spread like a disease. I have been told that this is a negative view, but I see them as a virus that spreads from evangelists and advocates. The secret is to stop the corporate immune system enveloping and supressing it.

Chapter 7

Step 6. Encourage break-out thinking

The question posed in this chapter is: 'Can everyone be creative and/or Innovative?' From the experience I have had over the last 12 years, working with many different types and ages of people, the answer I suggest is a most definite yes. People are born with an innate creative capability that is restricted as we grow older. Given the right tools and support, all of us can be creative and Innovative. So what are these tools?

When asked, most people say that being creative or Innovative takes a certain kind of person – that there is a 'type' of person whose DNA has the creativity gene. Indeed I thought the same for many years. I thought I was special: I had been singled out and given the gift of creativity. I remember seeking out personality profiling schemes such as Myers-Briggs and Belbin which proved to me that this was true – I was special!

In the Innovation Labs I worked with a wide variety of groups from senior management teams, government departments and operational teams through to schoolchildren and I realised I had been wrong all along. I wasn't special, I had just learned to be different!

I realised that given the right environment and stimulus everybody has the ability to be creative – and if they put their ideas into action, Innovative too. So what do I mean by environment and stimulus. I have covered many of the aspects of environment in Step 3 so I don't intend to go over them again in detail, other than to re-state the importance of removing self-limiting factors (things you perceive that you can't do or don't have permission to do, although in reality there are no such constraints) such as belief systems, environmental cues and company hierarchy/peer pressure from the equation.

The creation of a separate environment will for many be a luxury that cannot be justified or afforded. This should not stop you as individuals or as part of a company finding new and exciting places to hold your meetings and workshops. I have held some great workshops in nightclubs, cathedrals, narrow boats, fields and anywhere else I can find where people don't have cues about how to behave. My goal has always to been to run a workshop in an inflatable bouncy castle but I have never found a team that was willing to participate! I did once find a company in the USA who made inflatable offices and contacted I them with the idea of an inflatable Innovation lab, but never got the company I was working for to back the idea.

So what do I mean by break-out thinking? Many of us have adopted a 'learned' behaviour pattern that creates its own set of self-limiting beliefs. As babies we are born with no fears, no constraints. As we grow older we learn what is and is not acceptable, what danger is and how to behave. Typically we are told by our parents and peers what we are good at, and more importantly what we are not good at – whether this is true or not.

We then spend the rest of our lives trying to conform to this internal model we have of ourselves, our capabilities and limitations. I have known so many people who live a life of 'if-only' – all the things that they wanted to do but felt that they couldn't because of some abstract internal control mechanism.

Similarly, organisations have internal control mechanisms that limit their potential. There appears to be some form of learned corporate behaviour that restricts companies from fulfilling their promise. When questioned about these beliefs no one seems to know where they come from; they are just there. They are never written down and no one knows who started them – but everybody knows that they exist. They are passed down by word of mouth and all new entrants to the organisation seem to learn them within the first six months – sometimes a lot quicker. In this way the corporate immune system ensures that damage limitation is maintained.

Break-out thinking is therefore about trying to remove some of these internal controls and become what you and/or your company could be – achieving full potential.

Both creativity and Innovation require knowledge, information, stuff that the brain can process in the background. As I mentioned previously, I am intensely curious. I was the boy who spent time taking toys and packaging to pieces to see how it was made rather than playing with the toy itself. I have always been this way and have carried it on into my adult life. My garage is full of the remnants of hobbies I have been crazy about at some time or other, for once I had mastered the basics I would move on to the next.

Very often, interestingly, I would come back and move from the basics to become more adept at whatever it was at some point in the future. This curiosity is the basis, I believe, of Innovative/creative thinking as it provides the stimulus and raw information required to make the linkages that are the essence of Innovation. Being faced with an opportunity, or should I say problem, you can call on masses of data from all your sources – building the linkages that will bring new insight and new ideas to whatever it is.

Take the wind-up radio that was invented by Trevor Baylis. The story goes that back in 1993, he was watching a TV show about the spread of AIDS in Africa, and learned that in many parts of the continent radio was the only means of communication. But even a basic radio presented a major obstacle: the cost of batteries.

That simple fact set in motion a train of thought that eventually nudged him into his home workshop. A series of experiments led to a clockwork radio prototype that had to be wound up for two minutes and would run for 14 minutes. Somewhere in the back of his mind had been the principle of using springs as a power source, and he put two and two together and went away to invent the spring-powered radio, which has now sold over 3 million units worldwide, with over 150,000 being distributed into the poorer areas of Africa. Interestingly, rather than becoming the saviour of Africa the wind-up power source has become a highly sought-after gadget and probably serves most often as a conversation piece.

The wind-up concept has been taken into many other areas by the company set up to exploit the idea, with such devices as wind-up mobile phone chargers and torches. Nick Negroponte from MIT has developed a wind-up laptop computer, again aimed at children of the Third World. The 'one laptop per child' project aims to provide every child in the world with a wind-up laptop computer that will cost less than $100 to produce.

I hope you can see from this story the track of ideas that started way back in 1993 when Trevor Baylis was watching TV. He didn't have all the information in one place, but what he had in his mind was lots and lots of knowledge gathered over time about lots of subjects. He was able to assemble these ideas into something that has revolutionised people's lives by providing a sustainable power source. What is interesting is that the concept has be been built on and people have continued to Innovate around the subject of wind-up. Not in terms of the initial radio concept – that is, what else can I do with a radio – but seeing clockwork as a new power source, so that the question becomes what else could be powered in this way?

> The key to success is to risk thinking unconventional thoughts. Convention is the enemy of progress. As long as you've got slightly more perception than the average wrapped loaf, you could invent something.
>
> (Trevor Baylis, OBE)

So where did Trevor get his bank of ideas and knowledge in the first place? From interviews it appears he takes the time to expose himself to as much stimulus as possible, always seeking out the new and unusual.

For myself the place I get most ideas from is the media – magazines and periodicals which I consume at a great rate. As I mentioned previously they need to be as diverse as possible and each lasts me around an hour if it is really good – so, not a long attention span then!

An example of how reading a magazine article sparked a whole series of events is the story of a web-enabled postbox. I was reading a US magazine called *Popular Science* after one trip to America. It is as the title suggests a magazine for all branches of science, but it tends to feature some of the more obscure and can be a good source of ideas. In the magazine was an article about a company that had produced a web-server on a single chip (www.SitePlayer.com). The story was about a guy who had integrated the chip into his home alarm system. He could log on to the web server via his Internet-enabled mobile phone so that when he was in the pub he could find out when his wife got home and unset the alarm, and so he knew he'd better be making tracks back. Although this had no real parallel to my own situation (I wasn't married at the time), it was lodged as something of interest in the back of my mind.

A few weeks later I was out doing some 'frontline' work for a postal company in the UK and I was going around postboxes emptying mail. Although many of the postboxes were empty they still had to be visited at least once a day because there was no way of finding out if there was any mail in them other than by opening the door and looking. This triggered an idea: why couldn't we build a device that could monitor these boxes. The web-server chip article came back to me. There are over 10,000 of these boxes in the UK, so clearly cost was going to be a significant factor in any solution.

What if we could build a small, self-contained device that could record whether something had been posted and when the postbox had been visited? I set about ordering the various components I thought we might need from America, and set a small team up to see if what I had conceived was possible.

When I told the managers my great idea, their first response was that it would cost at least £2000 per postbox to install, and in many cases it would be would be impossible because there was no power in the vicinity of the postbox. I felt quite passionately that there was a germ of an idea here which had huge potential benefit for the company, so my response was to increase the pressure on the team by stating that the solution had to cost no more than £50 and should be totally self contained. After much protestation they went away to think again.

Each time the team came back, their proposition involved PCs or batteries the size of bricks. Then one day a colleague noticed that a parking meter in a remote village had been installed with a solar cell on the top to power it. I contacted the company that produced this device, and they sent me through a sample which was just right for our application. At the same time we obtained a data-only mobile phone. All the pieces of the jigsaw came together.

The team turned up in my office one day and showed me a prototype that they thought could be built for £40 – solar powered and using a stripped-down mobile phone for communications. In the end, however, the actual value that could be achieved was not sufficient for the project to go ahead. I think if it were revisited today, the falling cost of technology and the advent of 3G mobile technologies would change the cost–benefit ratio to positive. Although we unfortunately failed to convince the company that this was a viable idea and it never got off the ground, it proved my theory that everybody can be creative if given the correct stimulus.

This experience also taught me many lessons. It introduced me to the concept of *constraint* as a stimulus for creativity. What I had inadvertently done was stumble across another technique to get people's creative juices flowing – using (as it happened, false) constraints. I had set the constraint that the cost of the unit had to be no more than £50. It was clear to both myself and the team that this was an impossible figure to achieve using current thinking and would require a radical new approach. The first response was to question the constraint. However as time passed, the constraint (the £50 cost) became the answer and the question became how to achieve it. People had switched their thought pattern/process into achieving the impossible. Some of the ideas that came out along the way were pretty strange – involving clockwork mechanisms, weights and pulleys, and chickens or rats I seem to remember. But the constraint stimulated the team to discover new sources of knowledge and ideas.

After this experience I have tried this technique many times and have proved conclusively – at least to myself – that the technique works really well.

The second lesson from the experience was persistence: we had given up too early. If we had had the foresight to push the project on, I firmly believe that every postbox in the UK today would have these devices fitted. This raises another issue and potential lesson: we didn't care enough about the idea, it wasn't important enough for us and we didn't believe in ourselves. This is another factor that is very important when considering Innovation in a large company. We still got paid whether the idea came to fruition or not and there was no reward structure in place if it was successful – so we didn't really care.

Most organisations have a policy that any idea that people have while at work is the property of the company and the individual has no right over the intellectual property generated. The challenge, therefore, is how to get people to care enough about their ideas, to have enough passion, to bring them to a successful conclusion.

If we want people to be curious, to be Innovative, we have to make it worth their while. I don't just mean from a financial viewpoint but also from a psychological one. The psychological contract people enter into with their company is very different from any legal contract that may be in place. A psychological contract represents the mutual beliefs, perceptions and informal obligations between an employer and an employee. It sets the dynamics for the relationship and defines the detailed practicality of the work to be done. It is distinguishable from the formal written contract of employment as it is based on shared ideals and values, and is founded on 'mutual' respect and the support of both parties.

On a separate topic completely, I was listening to a radio programme afternoon on the subject of creativity and some learned US professor was discussing what was required for people to be creative. The three things she mentioned were space, time and stimulation – a catalyst for change, something that sparked an idea. I got to thinking again about the whole idea of social Innovation: using other people and their experience to stimulate innovation to take place. Is this a prerequisite for true Innovation to take place?

* * *

Step 6 is about encouraging break-out thinking, not only in your working life but in all aspects of your life. We all have the ability to be creative and innovative if we are given the right conditions and stimulus. The secret is to find out what works for you – what environment, what stimulus, whether you work best in a social situation or alone. Read as much as you can and expose yourself to as many external stimuli as possible. Look for ideas in everything you do: in the supermarket, in the press, on TV. Try and look at things differently – maybe through the enquiring eyes of a child.

We have discussed the idea of constraint, the ways people place false constraints on themselves and their thinking. A technique that can shake off the constrains is to constantly ask: "How could I do this twice as fast for half the cost?" Practise using this in your personal as well as your business life.

Chapter 8

Step 7. Learn to notice things differently

In the introduction I laid out the difference between creativity and Innovation. Creativity is a skill that can be taught although it requires a change of attitude, while Innovation is taking what you already know, your domain knowledge, and applying it in different ways. The common factor – and usually the reason why the two are linked – is the change in attitude that is required.

But what has this to do with looking at things differently? Well the change in attitude required for both creativity and Innovation typically changes the way you view the world, encourages you to be more curious and questioning. This should be encouraged both in yourself and in the people you come into contact with. At first people will look at you as though you are from a different planet, and figuratively you may very well be, but if you question the status quo this will eventually rub off and people will start their own journey of discovery. As I mentioned in the introduction, adopting the Innovative approach can change people's lives, and this needs to be considered early in the journey. I myself didn't realise what was happening until it was too late and I was divorced and living on my own. If I had been aware of the potential impact early in this period, I would probably have done things differently (yet looking back at this period, although it was painful at times, my life now is so much better than I thought it was destined to be before I started on the journey).

So how can you train yourself to notice things differently? I guess the secret is not to accept anything you see as normal, but try and view the world in a child-like (not childish) manner. Approach the world with wonder in your eyes. We have all tended to become very jaded with the familiar around us and it is not easy to change this. However, the benefits of this change are probably the biggest that can be gained from reading this book. I guess I liken it to being re-born, if that is not too much of a cliché. To see the world with new eyes, with wonder and excitement, is a very liberating experience and can be a life-changing event.

Increasing the amount of stimulation you receive can trigger this process by providing a range of different perspectives – particularly if you actively look for linkages between the different elements that you find. The scope of this stimulation is up to you and can encompass magazines and periodicals (my own favoured option), books of course, travel and extended contact with other people from all walks of life, all things that will give a wider range of perspectives. One technique I developed when reading magazines and periodicals which encouraged innovation was to take a random article or advertisement and look at how I or my company could use the product or idea. You might try that too, as well as thinking about how something you know or have could significantly help with a problem outlined in something you are reading – the more obscure the better. I call this technique MediaStorming and it is a good technique to use when trying to get teams to 'think outside the box': it forces you to take a different perspective.

Going back to the story about Trevor Baylis and the wind-up radio, this is exactly what he did. He saw a random TV programme on AIDS and used the knowledge and skill that he had built up elsewhere to solve the problem. He could have simply said 'I know nothing about AIDS, radios or communication,' but he didn't: he linked several pieces of information he had gained and came out with a revolutionary way of doing something. If he hadn't actively exposed himself to a wide range of information he wouldn't have had all the components necessary to build the linkages needed to solve this particular problem.

Try it yourself. Take a daily paper and randomly pick an article – preferably one that outlines a problem. It could be something about a death or murder, or a health problem or anything really. Then write the problem down at the top of a piece of paper. Underneath it write down all the things that you know about which might help solve the problem; the list will surprise you and will typically contain 30–50 items. Next, try to put together a solution from all the things you have listed.

You have now had your first experience of using your knowledge to solve a random problem. Try again. Pick another article and go through the process again; the more you do the easier it will become. After your third or fourth attempt you will start to apply it subconsciously to other problems you come across in daily life. Be careful not to take this too far, as it can become a little tiresome for your friends and colleagues – I know through bitter experience!

A different approach, which forces you to look at things differently, is a technique I developed early in my Innovation career: 'other people's shoes'. This technique forces you look at a problem, situation, issue or solution through the eyes of another person. Maybe not literally, but it does compel you to take a different perspective on things. This tool works really well with a jaded team who have looked at a particular issue many times, have arrived at 'stuck thinking' and keep coming up with the same stale solution that doesn't work.

The technique is to take four or more perspectives on the issue – maybe employer, employee, stakeholder and customer, or four contrasting age ranges or nationalities. A subsection of the participants take a particular group and go into a huddle to work out how that particular group/segment would view the situation. It may be necessary to provide some detail as to the age/sex of the customer but I have found that if you leave the group alone for a short while they prefer to decide themselves.

The individual viewpoints are then fed back to the whole group and recorded, in the Innovation labs typically on the walls but it could just as easily be done on paper or directly onto a computer. The strength of this technique is that it shows up the similarities and the differences from the alternative perspectives. A template for this technique is discussed in Appendix 4. Storytelling and role-play work extremely well as feedback mechanisms (See Appendix 3 for further details of storytelling).

Another technique adopted by some companies is to bring in outsiders – sometimes consultants, sometimes customers or even just 'strange' people to provide a completely different viewpoint on a situation, product or initiative. The benefit of this approach is that you get genuinely fresh views, particularly if you get the more 'obscure' individuals involved.

I have used an online anonymous brainstorming service for some years from Facilitate (www.facilitate.com) and Groupsystems (www.groupsystems.com) to bring in people from all over the world to provide fresh views. Both these services provide an anonymous brainstorming capability so you don't have a clue where the ideas and comments are coming from – an employee, a vagrant or a consultant! With the advent of the Internet and the World Wide Web, new tools and techniques are being developed on a daily basis. At the moment the two services mentioned above are the only ones that offer anonymous brainstorming, but it is only a matter of time before other sites appear that provide these types of services.

* * *

Noticing things differently is the topic of Step 7. The ability to look at the world through a different lens or through different eyes is something that you can become skilled at. We have all been 'trained' from our earliest days to see things in a certain way and this constrains our view of the world. Forcing yourself to see things from another perspective will give insights that will change your view of your life and your world.

Chapter 9

Step 8. Harvest ideas

As I mentioned early in the book, the techniques discussed could result in many ideas being generated. A typical 10–15-minute session using the active facilitation method and the anonymous brainstorming software in the Innovation Lab can generate over 300 ideas from a group of six to eight people – ideas are generated as fast as people can type. These are then grouped, refined, prioritised, developed and acted upon – with probably less than 10 per cent of the ideas being actually used in practice. So what about the other 90 per cent?

In the Innovation Lab environment we developed the ability to generate huge numbers of ideas – which was what we thought Innovation was all about – but unfortunately didn't develop the capability of turning them into bottom-line benefit. In the pilot Innovation Lab between 1998 and late 1999 we generated over 168,000 ideas – that is over 1600 ideas per week! Less than 0.000035 per cent of these actually turned into things that actually benefited the company. In fact there were just seven. What happened to the other 167,993? Were they all bad ideas? Were the ones that were chosen significantly better? No, but they tended to be the ones people were passionate about – which gave them a significant advantage over the others.

If 99.9 per cent are useful ideas that are not acted on, what can you do with them? Do you discard them and ignore the ideas that are in them? Well, that's we did in the early days – not realising the true value of what we had. The 'discarded' ideas have value in a number of ways. First, if there is a problem within a single company, these problem statements can be aggregated across a number of workshops and this can give an indication of bigger issues. If all the problems that come out in several workshops are about poor communications, morale or technology, then this is indicative of some root cause.

Second, although the ideas have been discarded, this doesn't make them bad ideas. It could be that someone was more passionate about the others, or that the timing was just not right. We developed a number of tools and techniques to harvest these ideas, which are discussed later in this chapter in more detail, so that we could try to 'recycle' them to find the gold nuggets. Typically, the first thing to do is just make sure you collect the ideas into some form of central repository. Many companies have suggestion schemes and idea-generation initiatives that usually produce hundreds if not thousands of ideas. They would expect 1 per cent or 2 per cent of these to be taken forward into an actual initiative. Few companies then store the others and look for patterns in them – which is where real value can be found. For some companies knowledge management was going to be the answer to this issue; in reality this seldom happens and the ideas are left to wither.

The Innovation fund which was discussed in some detail in Step 3, an internal venture capital fund of up to £4 million, at its peak generated many thousands of ideas – from small incremental improvements to operational practices through to major new technology-led initiatives which would potentially change the company. We designed the fund as a four-stage process that was 'gated' at each stage – further funding could be granted to take the idea to the next stage or funding could be withdrawn if the panel didn't think a project was worth taking further.

The difficult thing was to sort out which ideas to take forward, and to try and keep the decision-making panel as dispassionate as possible. How to distinguish the winners from the losers, the wheat from the chaff? Which are the ones that are certain to be winners? We had many ideas that were clearly not appropriate, but sometimes people were so passionate about them that they almost deserved to be given some money to at least flesh the ideas out.

If the ideas are not taken forward, the individuals who proposed them become disillusioned and will not make further contributions. The problem was not only how to pick the winners but what to do with the thousands of other ideas, which might be similar or address the same problem or be completely different. There may be some insight that could be drawn from this pool of ideas, or perhaps if a few of the ideas were combined then this would solve the problem at hand. This became a major task for the Innovation fund team: trying to get these insights and spot trends and so on as well as keeping people motivated to keep generating new ideas on a reasonably regular basis.

We approached a couple of universities to see if there was anything they knew about that would let us harvest the ideas. One of my team had been actively involved with Southampton University, which was looking at the idea of knowledge management from an analytical perspective. The university had developed an approach and some software that could read multiple Microsoft Word documents and look for patterns in the text – what words were near each other. (The project was known as Kermit, for some strange reason, and I am not sure if it is still a live initiative; although there is a web page it appears to be out of date.)

This technique was tried out on a contract with the Argentinean Post Office that a company had entered into. The university took all the emails and documents that had been produced by the project and ran them through its systems. The assumption was that the documents would contain lots of references to contracts, terms, letters, staff and other obvious matters. What actually came out was that much of the discussion in these documents was about horse blankets! Apparently much of the mail is still delivered on horseback to the more remote areas of Argentina, so horse blankets are highly important and there had been a problem sourcing suitable ones in the past.

This technique was applied to the many ideas that came out of the Innovation Lab and the Innovation fund. What came out was not rocket science and pointed to the fact that many of the problems that people were coming up with ideas for were to do with internal communications. If this sort of technique had not been employed this would never have come to light.

The concept of idea swarming was born. If the ideas generated by any initiative or series of initiatives – whether a suggestion scheme, workshop or brainstorming sessions – are analysed in totality, insights can be drawn from them. When I was running workshops in the Innovation Lab on a regular basis, we instinctively knew what the key issues were – what ideas and problems kept cropping up in each session.

One model I found useful was to map these ideas out on a chart using basic search techniques: namely, my brain! I would go through the Innovation fund ideas and, after an initial visual search to find if there were any obvious ones, I would look to code the ideas into one of four quadrants of a matrix: was the idea strategic or tactical, and would it have an internal or external focus? Using these four elements I would give the idea or problem a number and place it on the chart in a position that indicated the impact and size of the initiative/problem. If this was done for a series of creative problem-solving sessions, we could quickly see if there was a problem with a sales team or a particular product or service.

Similarly, if output from a range of brainstorming sessions is taken and analysed, it may become evident that 50 ideas are around suggestions for a particular service or way of working. That indicates that there may be something worth focussing on about that service or method. If it wasn't for this approach, those concepts might have been missed. In any single session, that topic might have been the subject of only one idea out of 300; even if the same idea kept coming up in a number of workshops it would not have been brought to the fore unless you undertook this type of analysis (or the same person facilitated every session).

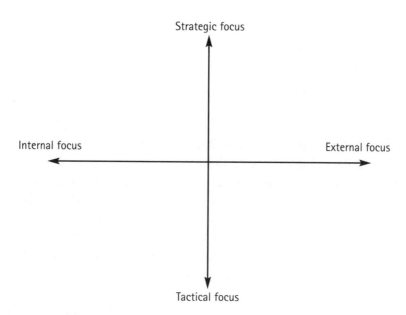

Figure 9 Idea-swarming matrix

Knowledge management was supposed to be the 'silver bullet' that was going to solve all our problems around the idea of gathering and analysing ideas. Although it was successful in a handful of companies in particular sectors where certain conditions applied, it has not solved the world's problems as the hype and the various consultancies involved in it suggested it would. I was knowledge management 'champion' for the company for a couple of years, and I know how hard it is for people to give up what they know and type it into the computer.

There is something deep in people's psyche which prevents them writing down their tacit knowledge – the stuff they know that they think keeps them in a job. For some this is true, but for most of us what we know is actually not that important; it is what we do with it that counts.

It is what we do with knowledge that counts

One of the large consultancies has recently opened up its research database, citing this as the reason. The fact that you know this stuff doesn't automatically mean that you know what to do with it – how to use it effectively in any situation.

In effect the opposite is true. The advent of the World Wide Web, and particularly search engines such as Google, has provided access to most of the world's knowledge at the touch of a button. Does this mean we can solve all our problems now we know everything? Of course not. If you don't know how to apply the information you have or don't have part of the information to complete the 'jigsaw', having access to the information is meaningless. For many, access to all this information has just confused the situation because they now have too much information which they cannot process, or in some cases comprehend. Access to all this information also raises an issue for the academic establishments that are trying to understand their strengths: what will their role be in the future?

So how do you ensure that you 'harvest' the best ideas from the thousands that will be kicking around the company? Well the first thing to do is to actively capture them, then define a 'process' for categorising them – segmenting them by customer, supplier, processing and so on. Then look to identify the things that are stopping them being great ideas, the factors that are inhibiting somebody from taking them forward. Lastly identify the potential impact and costs of the idea. All this can be captured simply in an Excel spreadsheet and then the various columns can be sorted to identify the 'swarms' of ideas around a particular theme, or barrier or impact.

* * *

In Step 8 I have covered harvesting the ideas that are around us, either written down somewhere, on a database or in people's heads. Many of these ideas go unnoticed or are never brought to the surfaced and therefore are wasted. There will probably be the 'golden nugget' of an idea that could bring dramatic benefits somewhere within the company or its people if only it could be found!

How you know if something is a good idea or not is also discussed, as is the need to provide some form of analytical framework to assess the benefit and impact of any idea on you or the company. The need to have a repository for these ideas is also discussed, although this needs to be implemented in a simple way – the more complex it is, the less likely it is to be maintained and updated.

Chapter 10

Step 9. Develop a new way of working

The normal way of working typically becomes invalid when you are trying to be Innovative or creative in a corporate environment. As discussed previously, the corporate immune system will try to suppress any disruptive activities and unsettling behaviour; it will try to maintain the status quo within the company. I have seen many examples of highly creative and innovative people being sidelined or forced to comply with the company norm – fit in or get out! This attitude has resulted in a sterilisation of companies where a norm is established and then reinforced by the stories that make up the culture of the company.

In the late 1990s the company I was working for undertook a psychological profiling exercise of over 1500 senior managers using the Myers-Briggs (www.myersbriggs.com) preference profiling. At the time, over 80 per cent of the people analysed were 'ISTJ'; these are people who are introverts (I) who prefer detail (S), have logical minds (T) and are more comfortable taking small incremental steps (J). Only 5 per cent of the company had a radically different profile – the extroverts who could work with concepts and visualise different futures (ENTP; people who are extroverted (E), intuitive (I), thinking (T) and perceiving (P)). This group typically didn't fit into the corporate norm. The recruitment techniques employed at the time sought out people who would not challenge the culture of the company, who would comply with the psychological contract that the company wanted rather than challenge it.

Although the Myers-Briggs technique is targeted at individuals, the concept of company profiles has recently become a topic of discussion and a number of conferences have started to be advertised in this area. So the question arises. Do different types of companies have different profiles? And if so, are these consciously created or are they in fact the result of a number of seemingly random actions. Are service companies more likely to recruit into one mould and a product company into another? Can a company profile be changed or is this linked to the corporate culture?

There are many other organisational models that could be used, and I am sure that there are a number of consultancies that will undertake the analysis for you.

Process

Process or politics

A couple of questions have been on my mind recently as I have been researching this book and talking to a wide range of people on the subject. The first question is: Is innovation a process – a linear progression of activities that will lead to an output?

I will try and answer this by looking at the various models that are used in industry today – and there are many to look at! Most of the models are a four or five-stage 'funnel' where many ideas are funnelled down through a number of gated stages that weed out the ideas that won't make it. I will also tap into my experience of using these models over the last 12 years and hopefully provide some insight into what is important and what is not.

Trawling the Internet, and working with the many consultancies out there, shows that there are thousands of Innovation process models and frameworks – each valid in its own right and effective for some companies. Many of these, as previously mentioned, employ some form of funnelling technique, which is gated at each stage to allow for selection or rejection of ideas. Some of these frameworks have as few as three stages, but I have seen others with as many as eight. The one we developed for the last company I worked for is shown below; it is a four-stage gate process to filter out the ideas that didn't fit. This highlights the first problem with this approach.

In this staged-gate process the organisation has four opportunities to squash any idea that is disruptive or not considered 'strategic'. The

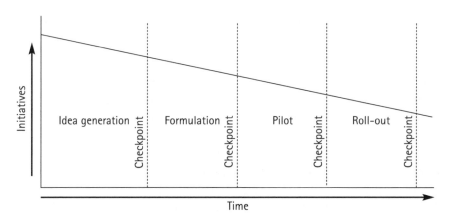

Figure 10 The four-step approach

approach also relies on a steady stream of ideas being available on a regular basis from whatever source is appropriate. However human nature is such that if none of your ideas are getting through then you will eventually stop putting them forward.

The second issue with this approach is that of ownership – who controls the process. The people who have to implement the ideas typically own it in many organisations. These individuals or teams are not usually creative people but 'deliverers' whose task is to take the great ideas out of the process/framework and turn them into reality. In one year over 2000 ideas went into the Innovation process and zero turned into reality. It was not that the ideas were bad, it was just that they didn't fit into the current company strategy. Among them were some truly great ideas that other companies have since developed and that are now producing significant profits. Simple ideas that could have transformed procedures and slashed costs were dismissed because 'That's not how we do things', or because they were 'not aligned with the company's vision and strategy', or in some cases because they threatened some particularly powerful individual within the company or fell foul of 'turf wars'.

Yes, I sound bitter, and I guess I am. I have seen so many potentially great ideas go down this road and be dismissed for seemingly spurious reasons, only to see other, usually smaller, companies pick them up and run with them and make serious money. On a couple of occasions I have also seen the company that rejected an idea buy the company that made it a success – ironic isn't it?

It is not in the owning group's interest for the ideas to be too disruptive or wacky as it will make their task more difficult or in some cases impossible, so they ensure that only 'compliant' ideas get through the system. This is the corporate immune system in action. Once Innovation becomes a process it means that it can go off the corporate radar, as it becomes someone's 'responsibility'. Another effect of this is that Innovation becomes somebody's job and the rest of the company or team shrug off their responsibility to Innovate. The real challenge and the concept of the 10-step approach and sticky Innovation are to make it everyone's responsibility to Innovate right through the company, not just a person or a team of people.

Solitary or social

The second and more recent question is: Is Innovation a solitary or social activity?

This is an interesting question and one that I hadn't really thought about until I was chatting to an ex-colleague who I was starting to do some work with. She started a conversation about where people had the best ideas, and recalled how that morning she had been driving a bus of elderly people for a local charity when suddenly she had had this great idea. Not that she was thinking about anything in particular but she had had a problem in the back of her mind for some time. When we met she talked it through and I added a few ideas and comments, and then she went off to implement it. This experience got me thinking about where and when great ideas 'appear' – as that is what they seem to do. It is as if when you least expect it, the solution to a particular problem just seems to come out of the blue.

One school of thought is that your mind taps into some form of super-consciousness, a 'melding' of minds at some ethereal level. My own view is that we use only a small part of the brain much of the time, and it is when we allow some of the lower functions – the more intuitive and creative parts – to engage on a problem, then this is the time we get those 'eureka' moments.

For me, the place I have some of my best ideas is in the bathroom, particularly in the bath, I guess because it is a place of solitude and reflection. One of the other great things about the bathroom is that very often you have a handy whiteboard – either wall tiles or mirrors! I always have dry-wipe pens in the bathroom, although I have to be careful not to get the pen in between the tiles as it doesn't wipe off – a fact that my wife is all too aware of!

The other place for ideas is the car – again a place of solitude and reflection – although hopefully you are concentrating on driving! Here again a whiteboard is available in the form of windows – although I have taken to travelling with a voice recorder, as it is safer. You certainly get some strange looks writing on windows at traffic lights and I am not sure what the law would say on the subject – is this dangerous driving or having ideas without due care and attention!

This question of social or solitary got me thinking about whether I had had a great idea when I was working in a team environment – in a social space. The answer was probably yes, although the idea would typically have built upon somebody else's thoughts or ideas.

But can Innovation be social or do you need solitude and refection to bring your experience and knowledge to bear on a problem or opportunity. I looked back at some of the tools and techniques we had developed over the last 12 years and realised that actually what we were encouraging and catalysing was *social Innovation*. We were, inadvertently I guess, creating an environment where teams – unencumbered by environmental stimulus – could Innovate. Of course if you delve into social Innovation you need to carefully consider the Intellectual property issues and make sure these are ironed out prior to any 'engagement' of the team. However techniques such as media storming, 'make it real' and 'other people's shoes' all provide a framework for social Innovation (details of these techniques are contained in Appendix 4).

So how does social Innovation work? The team should have a clear and unambiguous understanding of what the problem or issue is that is to be addressed. Ideally this should be communicated before the event – to allow a little solitary Innovation to ferment. Time should be given for individuals to share their individual thoughts with others. One facility that could be used here is the whiteboard wall. Each individual writes his or her idea on a post-it note or card and sticks it on the wall; the ideas are roughly grouped and then linkages are drawn between ideas that have common 'DNA' or characteristics. The group is then asked to stand back and think about what is on the wall – hopefully this will start the social Innovation juices flowing. New cards should be written that bring together elements of the cards already on the wall, and new linkages created. After three or four cycles the number of new cards will be reducing and the ideas distilled to the two or three really great ideas.

How does this differ from solitary Innovation? When individuals take on a problem or task and are asked to Innovate around it, they have only limited knowledge with which to build the links that are required to Innovate. By socialising this activity you are exposing the problem to the total knowledge and experience of the group. As mentioned previously, the intellectual property issue needs to be tackled up front, as one of these ideas could make a million and serious legal and financial issues could emerge. Whose idea was it and what would be the consequences of success?

Taking the ideas forward is best done in solitary mode, as it needs the personal vision, passion and drive to carry the idea into reality. People who make things happen typically have an entrepreneurial spirit, a wide network of contacts and information sources, and the enthusiasm and vision to get over the many setbacks that are almost certain to befall the project. It took Dyson something like 15 years to get his bagless vacuum cleaner from concept to reality, and the personal and financial costs of that must have been huge. He is now lionised as a lucky guy who made the break from convention – the fact that it took 15 years is forgotten.

I once remember someone telling me 'You know the harder I work the luckier I get.' Innovation is not something that happens overnight; it does take persistence, patience and particularly passion to take an idea from concept to reality.

* * *

Developing new ways of working is discussed in Step 9, along with the need to do things differently. Whether or not we are engaged in Innovative activities, we should all strive to improve the things we do on a personal, team or company basis. The current business focus on efficiency and cost cutting, brought about by the pressures of globalisation, competition and technology, is forcing companies to strive for continual improvement. Engagement of frontline staff in the process, through quality circles and Workout methods, has been proved to improve the 'stickiness' of any change activity dramatically.

The question is raised as to whether Innovation is a social or solitary activity, and the answer I give is 'both'. In the early stages of formulating your thoughts the social factors are important, providing stimulus; the consolidation of the idea, however, is usually a solitary event. For different people the balance between social and solitary will be different – some people will require more solitude and some less.

Chapter 11

Step 10. Benchmark and measure

As Innovation is a rather esoteric concept, it is a difficult thing to measure. The outputs of Innovation are rather easier, although proving the connection between an idea and a delivered output can at times be difficult. Successful ideas generate many parents and benefactors – all wanting to claim ownership.

There are several factors, which can influence this, with time being one of the most important. For an idea to move from a concept to a reality typically takes 12–14 months, which in a large, relatively fast-moving business can be a lifetime. I have known whole teams break up and new management teams form in less time than it takes an idea to go through a four/five-stage gated process. This gestation period is therefore an issue as the sponsors, individuals, budgets and market can all change in the time it takes to get authority to move to the next stage.

Another factor is the area of budgets, as typically the operational unit that may implement the initiative or idea needs to claim the initiative to meet its financial targets and no recognition is given to the Innovation activity as this would lessen the benefit to the operational group. These factors lead companies to view Innovation measurement in a particular light. There is a need to prove the value of any Innovation activity, typically with a short, 12–18 month period. This leads to very tactical, short-term, small 'i' activities rather than the long-term strategic approach which is arguably necessary for long-term survival.

One of the basic issues when trying to measure Innovation is to understand what the baseline is. Improvement can only be measured if you know where you are starting from. When a balanced-scorecard approach has been introduced into a company, there is typically much pressure to produce 'meaningful' measures of Innovation performance. Unfortunately, due to the esoteric nature of Innovation, quantitative measures – which are very often introduced retrospectively – can be meaningless or at worst destructive. They can introduce spurious activity aimed at achieving the measure rather than actually innovating anything!

'You are what you measure' is as true for Innovation as it is for any other business discipline

The three types of metrics which are most commonly applied to innovation are:

- *Output*: this is the most frequently measured, perhaps because it tends to be the easiest. Typical metrics in this area are number of ideas generated, number of ideas turned into reality, perceived quality of ideas, number of ideas per person/per team, and money value.
- *The process of Innovation*: the number of ideas at each stage of the Innovation process and how these ideas are implemented. This is usually measured at the stage gates in a typical four or five-stage gate process.
- *The consequences of Innovation*: has the company changed, has it become inherently Innovative? For me this is the most important measure of the value of Innovation, although in reality it is also the hardest to measure.

To address the baseline issue in the company I worked for, the concept of an Innovation audit was developed and a questionnaire produced for circulation around a significant community within the company (see Appendix 1). This questionnaire sought to assess the current state of Innovation within the company, and again to try and ascertain the barriers perceived by the interviewees to the exploitation of ideas within the organisation. In parallel to this a questionnaire was circulated through a UK-based business school to 40 companies around the UK.

What was interesting from the UK company sample was that few organisations had developed any level of sophistication in the measurement of Innovation. Out of the 40 companies contacted, only six responded, with many of them focussing on product development: number of ideas generated, value generated post implementation and, for those companies with a stage gate process, how many projects are at each stage. It was fascinating to see, however, that none of the companies reported on these metrics with any rigour.

In the absence of any accepted Innovation measurement methodology or practice we decided to develop our own metrics, which would be pertinent to the company's current situation. These metrics would focus around the exploitation of the ideas and the value generated by them.

A possible balanced scorecard therefore for Innovation has three measures:

- *Success stories*: these are one-page 'stories' of how the Innovation has added value or contributed to a particular project or initiative. These stories are typically endorsed by an operational unit director or one of the unit's team, and are produced in a standard format. In one year we managed to produce around 16 of these, which were put on the intranet and submitted to the management team as proof of the value of the Innovation team. This focus on added value created a very different atmosphere in the Innovation unit as exploitation of ideas become the focus rather than just idea generation.
- *New products and services*: to encourage the team to continue their research activities, a second measure was put in place that focussed on the number of new product/service ideas generated. This showed the percentage increase on the previous years figures.
- *Innovation audit*: how innovative do staff feel the company is? This was included in the annual 'Have your say' employee questionnaire.

In the 12 years I have been involved with Innovation, the measurement of activities in this area has changed as the needs of the company and the environment it operates in have developed. It appears from the research undertaken that there is no one simple answer to the question, but there are potential solutions. The deployment of a tool such as the Innovation audit on a regular basis within an organisation should produce a sense of how the organisation is changing over time. This, coupled with a small number of quantifiable measures of ideas generated and ideas taken into action, should provide a company with a year-on-year measure, an Innovation index which will allow them to ascertain the value of activity in this area and also to benchmark themselves against other companies and market sectors.

* * *

This last step covers the need for benchmarking and measurement, which are vital to ensure continued support and ultimate success in whatever your venture is – whether personal or business.

The measures should however be realistic and appropriate to the task in hand. Traditional business measures are too often placed on non-traditional activities, causing the idea or whatever it is to be quashed by the measure. These traditional measures tend to be whatever the flavour of the month is – whether that is the balanced scorecard, traffic light system or some other consultancy-induced fad. To force these measures on a small start-up activity can be the kiss of death as they stifle the team, and very often never reflect the targets, whatever they are. I have had situations where some great ideas have been killed because they wouldn't turn over £100m in five years and therefore were wasting management time – an arrogant approach if ever there was one.

This chapter has discussed new ways of measuring Innovation, which need to be tailored to your particular organisation or situation. These measures should be widely publicised to ensure the 'dance of Innovation' is reinforced, and that commitment and support are maintained.

Chapter 12

The people aspects of Innovation: attitude vs. knowledge vs. skill

The people aspects of Innovation are again reinforced in his chapter.

Attitude, knowledge and skill

The concept of using the three elements of attitude, knowledge and skill has been employed in the training, mentoring and education fields for some time. The concept of applying these three dynamics to Innovation and creativity is discussed in detail in this chapter.

The three elements are important when considering the people elements of any Innovation initiative – whether it be a small 'i' incremental change programme such as Workout or the use of quality circles, or a big 'I' radical Innovation programme, setting up an Innovation team or embarking on a company culture change initiative. The dynamics of these three elements need to be properly considered when undertaking any one of these activities.

Skill

Skill is what you have learned, what you have been taught. Small children gain new skills almost on a daily basis. As we grow older the take-up of new skills slows down but we always have the ability to

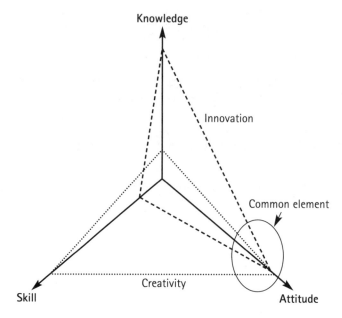

Figure 11 Skills, knowledge and attitude

learn, although we often choose not to. A skill can be taught; it is something that you can be instructed in. Whether you are good at it depends on your approach and how much effort you put into the learning process. I have taught creativity and creative thinking for over 10 years and have learned that it is indeed a skill, something that people can learn how to do. I haven't met anyone who cannot be creative; given the right set of tools everyone can become skilled in how to use them as long as they are prepared to change their attitude and let themselves be creative.

Knowledge

This is similar to skill, in that it is something that is continually acquired from childhood. We all have knowledge and it is all different. The wealth of knowledge I have is completely different from anybody else's in the world. The experiences I have gone through, the travel I have done, the people I have met, the jobs I have undertaken and the books and magazines that I have read have all contributed to my unique set of knowledge. No two people can ever have the same set of knowledge.

The more knowledge we have, the more opportunity there is to build linkages and therefore be Innovative. For myself I have always been intensely curious and an avid reader, not of books particularly but of magazines and periodicals, although much can also be learned from history – in fact many of the dot-com millionaires had history qualifications.

I believe it is easier to translate today's thinking into today's solutions to your problem. I currently subscribe to over 15 magazines – my postman must hate me – on a wide range of topics – and yes I do read my wife's magazines too although I don't usually admit to that! All these are food for new ideas to build linkages between the problems and issues I face today and their potential solutions. The 'media-storming' technique refines this knowledge acquisition and linking and is described in further detail in Appendix 4.

Attitude

Now we come to the most difficult element to explain – attitude. As with knowledge, each person's attitude is different from anybody else's. Attitude is your approach to life, how you view things, how you interact with people, your values and beliefs and how you respond to certain situations; to some degree it governs the sort of jobs you have, the relationships you get into, and some would argue the success you have in your life. One question that I have been asked on a number of occasions is: Can attitude be changed? Of course it can; but the deeper question is – how long for? How deeply engrained is attitude?

Attitude is formed from an early age and by a wide variety of social, educational and cultural stimuli. Children tend to have a very open attitude up to the age of between five and seven, and then they start to take on the elements that will stay with them for life As the child grows older it becomes harder to change the basic elements of attitude. In later life it is very difficult as social and peer pressures dictate a hardening of attitude, particularly for men as they are expected to operate in a 'macho' way; it typically requires a very conscious effort to make the changes needed to become truly Innovative and creative.

Innovation and creativity

Let us now consider the dynamics of these three elements when applied to Innovation and creativity. What are the dynamic factors? Let's look at creativity first.

Creativity

Creativity, I would suggest, is a real skill. I can teach you how to be creative. I can provide a set of tools and techniques that will allow anybody to be creative. These tools and techniques have been developed and refined for thousands of years and will continue to develop in the future.

For the purposes of this book I do not intend to look at the creative arts such as drawing and painting, as this is something I am not qualified to discuss. I have had forays into this area with some limited success, but there are literally thousands of books on the shelves that will help you master these skills. I have used creative arts in workshop situations, as this is something that helps people to start to realise that they are actually creative, and it can be a very liberating experience. To find out that they can paint, play the drums and dance if shown the right technique can really change people's lives, and I would encourage you to try at least one new creative art every year. You may not be good at all of them, or indeed any of them, but the mere fact that you are exposing yourself to these new stimuli will add to your creative ability in other areas of your life.

When creativity is applied to solving problems there appear from my research to be five ways to stimulate creative thinking. If you undertake a Google search you will find many thousands of techniques listed, and if you look again tomorrow more will have been added. Does this mean that you have to learn all these techniques? Well, no. I believe that all you have to learn are the five types, which you can then use as guides to create your approach – your own way of doing things. The five types of creative tools are:

- Parallels: looking for parallels with other topics/areas.

- Inversion/reversals: turning the problem or parts of the problem upside down.
- Randomness: introducing random stimulation through pictures, words and so on.
- Disassembly: looking at the component parts of the problem and analysing them.
- Constraints: introducing false constraints – half the cost, half the size, twice as fast and so on.

These approaches can be applied to many if not all situations. Consider a problem that is focussed upon the loss of revenue from a particular product stream with a particular customer. Using the above five approaches the following could apply:

- Parallels
  - What other companies are operating in this area?
  - Are they approaching things differently?
  - Who else is selling into the target customer base?
  - What approaches are they using?
  - Is there an approach in another industry/sector that you could use?
- Inversion
  - How could we stop selling to the customer?
  - Could we cease the product stream or source it elsewhere?
  - What if the product suddenly became a top seller?
- Randomness
  - How could the problem be solved using a random article?
  - Use a picture of a tree to stimulate thought – new branches, solid roots, acorn metaphor (small activity creates huge output) etc.
  - Use a random article in a magazine and look at how the product could help/hinder us.
  - Use a random word such as aardvark, and see if this stimulates any ideas.
- Disassembly
  - Who is the real customer?
  - Why does the customer use this product?
  - What need is the product satisfying?

- – What is the product used for? What else could be used?
    - – How much revenue is lost? What are the associated costs?
- Constraints
    - – What would happen if the product weren't available?
    - – How could we double the revenue from this customer?
    - – How could we halve the price of the product?
    - – How could we make the product half the size?

A list of tools and techniques to help you is contained in Appendix 4.

To apply these skills, however there needs to be a change in attitude. Most people when asked whether they are creative or not will probably answer no. They have a self-limiting belief that they aren't the creative type – but who is? They may have experienced failure in the past or they may have been told that they are not creative or they may just never have been given permission to be creative. This latter factor is one of the most likely reasons for this belief.

When I ask teams to be creative – draw a picture, build a model, write a story or some other task – the first response is nearly always: 'I can't do that, I am not creative.' After some encouragement and prompting however, they produce results that are amazing. There is some latent creative element in all of us and for many it is just a question of releasing it by giving it permission to come out, to show.

Innovation

Let's move on to Innovation. Innovation, I believe, cannot be taught as such. Innovation is about using your knowledge and applying it in different ways to new situations. There are techniques that can help you be Innovative and frameworks that can provide a guide for you, but there is no specific factor other than the knowledge you have and a change in attitude.

The thing that joins creativity and Innovation therefore is a change in attitude, and many of the steps in this book are around encouraging you to start a journey that will change your attitude for life. It is true that people usually first approach Innovation, as I did, through creativity, as this is something that can be learned and is a powerful catalyst to changing your attitude – this common factor between Innovation and creativity.

So what can you do to change people's attitude? Well it depends on whether you want to change one person's attitude or that of the whole company. You also need to try and understand why people would want to change in the first place. I will deal with each of these areas separately, although you will see that there is similarity between the two groups – after all a company is just a set of individuals!

Attitude change

Individual attitude change

From my own experience over the last 12 years I believe the best way to change personal attitudes – particularly towards Innovation and creativity – is to give people permission to be themselves: to allow the inner them to come to the fore.

Most of the personal development programmes by people such as Anthony Robbins and Brian Tracey relate to this permission giving – believe me I have bought into most of them at some time in my life. I have stood in front of a mirror and told myself how wonderful I am more times than I care to mention or admit to.

We all are constrained by our self-limiting beliefs, which have been built up since we were seven or eight years old. These beliefs, often irrational and foolish, stop us from becoming 'whole' beings. They also stop us being creative and at times innovative: we believe we are not creative and cannot be innovative. I am here to tell you that you are and you can!

So how do you change your belief system? Well you can pay good money to the many life gurus that offer to change your life or you can do it yourself and – stealing a phrase from Nike – *just do it!*

Organisational attitude change

When considering tactics for organisational attitude change, the first thing to consider is what you are trying to achieve. Make sure you are honest when undertaking this piece of analysis. Getting this right is vital as it will be difficult to correct things at a later stage. Unleashing massive creativity can be significantly disruptive to a company and can unbalance an organisation's ability to perform in its markets. Similarly with Innovation – creating a truly innovative company, something that many people talk about, may sound good in theory but in reality it can be highly disruptive.

Going back to the discussion we had in the very first chapter of this book and the definition of Innovation, having lots of people coming up with either little 'i' or even worse big 'I' Innovations can result in a dysfunctional company. In this respect it is better to try and constrain it and have a tapered rollout over a period of time.

Let's assume you have understood the risks and decided where you are trying to get to – How do you actually do it? The first step is to plan any initiatives very carefully, bringing together a focussed team to oversee the change. Many organisations at this stage would bring in external consultancies, assuming this will mitigate some of the risks as they will have done things like this before. Although on the surface this can seem to be a low-risk option, it could prove otherwise as the consultants will walk away at the end of a predefined period and you will be left to pick up the pieces.

A more rational approach is to use consultancies to train and mentor your own people, and then use them and only them to execute the initiatives. This approach is more likely to gain buy-in from staff and hopefully provide a level of 'stickiness' to the programme.

It is important that the communications for the initiative are well managed and planned carefully. The balance of internal and external media coverage is also important, bearing in mind that the potential positive impact of positive external coverage will attract the much-needed senior management support and hopefully engender pride in the workforce – reinforcing the change itself.

Within the organisation a reward and recognition system should be developed that supports the characteristics and behaviours you are looking for. This can be difficult for large organisations as many of these characteristics can be intangible – and therefore difficult to measure (these are covered in more detail in Step 10).

Chapter 13

Putting it all together

So what does it all mean? I have spent the last chapters explaining my experience over the last 12 years. I have provided lots of lessons, examples and tools and techniques, which I hope you found interesting. If you got this far I guess it wasn't such a bad journey. But how can you use all this new knowledge and skill? In this chapter, I look at two scenarios and set out an example journey for each. The first is the big Innovation initiative the management team decides to embark on, and the second is a new strategic goal for the company or team.

Scenario I: the big initiative

It is Tuesday morning. It's 10:30 am and your boss walks up to your desk and tells you that at the board meeting yesterday it was decided that the company had to have an Innovation initiative. A report in the *Sunday Times* stated that one of your biggest competitors had attributed its significant increase in share price to its Innovation team, which had been responsible for eight new products over the last six months and had reduced costs by 17 per cent.

So what do you do? Of course because you have read this book you know the first thing is to ask: 'What do you mean by Innovation? What does the board expect of this new initiative? How will they know if it is successful?' It is likely that the response will be a blank look and then some waffle about survival, culture change and other management speak. Of course you will persist, as you know that unless you understand your destination it is no good starting out on your journey.

Step 1. Understand where you are going

The first thing you suggest is that you get the Board together in a day-long workshop to work through their thoughts. This will be a difficult thing to arrange, but that will be your first opportunity to put your passion, patience and persistence to the test. After a lot of work, you have your workshop arranged for two weeks' time. What next?

An approach, which I favour, is to 'pick-off' the board members who will be attending on a one-to-one basis to brief them on the initiative and also try to understand any 'politics' that may or may not hinder the initiative and, more importantly, this first event. This can be a little bit of a challenge, particularly if it is 'not their party' – and some will certainly be cynical as they will have seen so many of these types of initiative before.

The first thing you need to sort out is the framework for the day and any preparatory work they need to do that they should bring along to the session. (It is likely that at least 20 per cent of the people scheduled to attend will have 'more important' meetings to attend so it is important that you get at least some input from them.)

The preparatory work should aim to bring out their 'innermost' thoughts and feelings as well as the things that are causing them sleepless nights. Not all of this will be relevant but they will find it cathartic and it will force them to take time out to think. I suggest that the pre-work should ask questions such as:

Imagine the Innovation initiative has been the most successful thing the company has ever done:
- What would a typical day be like?
- What would people be talking about?
- What would the analysts be saying?
- What would the competition be saying?
- What would the press be saying?
- What would the lead story on the intranet site be?

I suggest that you provide them with a framework to structure their thoughts and to ensure that you get a standardised input into the session. Tell them (I was going to say ask them, but I have found that if you ask their permission then they are likely to say no – as I wrote earlier it is easier to ask for forgiveness than permission) to make the documents anonymous and then either put them on a website that they can access, email them or send paper copies round.

The latter is probably the most effective as it is something that they can take with them and write notes on. With luck you will have these dossiers prior to the session, and I suggest you look for similarities and differences – see if you can put together a story or image of life in this new world. This will be used as input to the workshop and will be the first exercise you will ask them to undertake.

The workshop itself should be held away from the office, some-where that will provide either a degree of isolation or some visual stimulus. The session would typically last one or two days and should definitely include an overnight stay, as this is where much of the discussion and development of ideas will take place. Try to time the workshop for the middle or early part of the week (early and they don't get the chance to go in to the office, middle and they have the chance to do other things at either end). Last, and probably most difficult to enforce, is the 'No mobile phone or Blackberry' rule. I have been in a number of meetings recently where there is a sub-meeting going on via texted email, which can not only be disruptive to the meeting but makes it very difficult for people to follow what is happening around them!

On the day of the workshop, make sure you are well prepared – this session will be the one that they all remember and will set the 'tone' for future Innovation activities. If you don't feel confident facilitating the event, it may be worth getting in a professional facilitator. Make sure that whoever you get is prepared to do it your way, as many will see this as an opportunity to get a foot in the door and want to prove how 'wonderful' they are.

Finally do try and make sure that the venue isn't somewhere that they would expect it to be. Contact details for the Innovation labs around the UK are contained in Appendix 3 if you want to experi-ence one of these facilities; if not find somewhere a bit different. Many museums, visitor attractions, nightclubs and even some churches have rooms to rent, and as they are not frequently used by business tend to be significantly cheaper than the more traditional hotels and similar venues. (You may have to organise refreshments but there are plenty of shops and small businesses that would be more than happy to supply catering.)

An agenda/framework for the workshop could look something like:

Welcome and admin etc.

Positioning	Why we are having the workshop, company performance etc.
Understanding the future	Build a timeline of all the things you know about that will be important over the period being considered in the workshop.
Visioning	Where do we want the company to be: – financially – market positioning – customers – etc?
Living the vision	Create scenarios for the different futures, perhaps using 'other people's shoes' or one of the other techniques. Consider the use of media storming to stimulate radical ideas and thoughts. Maybe use the 'future news' template to write your own news headlines.
Feedback the ideas	Use stories, rich pictures and other ways of bringing the visions to life.
Discussion	Establish how you are going to decide which of the futures, or which elements of the futures, the team can buy into.
Timelining	Revisit the timeline to add in the steps you will need to take to bring your vision alive.

Action plan

A vital step is to decide what is going to happen next – ideally within a short period of time. Of course the 'who' is also important, and the definition of the resources required to make whatever it is happen.

Step 2. Where are you now?

After the workshop you have a clearer understanding of what the company is trying to achieve through this Innovation initiative. The next step is to understand where you are in comparison with this new vision. The Innovation audit questionnaire is contained in Appendix 1 for you to use and or modify. This should be used across a wide as group as possible, and at all levels across the organisation or across the particular section (marketing, operations or whatever) to get an understanding of the current state of play.

The circulation of this questionnaire can also be used as an opportunity to launch the Innovation initiative within the company – to start the 'dance of Innovation' (see Step 5). Use the opportunity to lay out some of the vision gained from the Step 1 workshop if the team will allow it.

How Innovative the company or team is will be evident from the type of targets and objectives people have – how many of them are about having great ideas, improving efficiency and similar themes, and how many are about delivery?

My guess is that over 90 per cent of the objectives and targets will be about the latter – the delivery of things – rather than the development of new property, or ideas. As time goes by this seems to be becoming an increasing trend: there is increasing focus on delivery, presumably due to the increased pressure brought about by globalisation and the Internet. What is probably actually needed is to do things very differently rather than attempting to increase efficiency. Going back to the adage 'you are what you measure', however, it would appear that the majority of UK companies are striving for that mythical efficiency nirvana.

So in this scenario the first thing we need to find out is where we are now, in terms of the company, the customer and the people involved. This will probably involve some detailed analysis of information, and what will probably surprise you is that some of the most basic information will not be easily available. I may be wrong but certainly my experience reinforces this.

Step 3. Create the right environment

For this scenario the right environment will depend on the approach taken by the individuals involved. It will probably consist of a number of strands, the first being the physical environment. One method of creating a physical environment or space may be to create a 'war room' – a designated area or room that a team of people can use to pull all the information together and work in for short periods of time.

Clearly there will be need for funding and resources, and it will be the sponsor's responsibility to make sure these are in place. Ideally the sponsor should be a director or senior manager who is influential within the company and respected by the senior management. Without this support the initiative may flounder as the 'oxygen' that allows the initiative to breathe will be denied, suffocating the activities.

The topic of resources will also be a contentious one within the organisation. The success of the solution you are seeking will be vital to the future of the company, and therefore the best people should be put on the project. However what usually happens is that they may stay with the project for the first couple of days but then something else comes up and they are sent to fight another fire elsewhere. By the end of the week the Innovation initiative has been weakened to such an extent that there is no way it can succeed – again starved of the 'oxygen' it needs to survive.

I have seen this happen so many times, and of course it is never recognised at the time. The kind of people that are required for the initiative are of course scarce within any company and there will be many demands on them. But if the project is really important to the company, the sponsor must make sure that headroom is provided to let success happen.

Lastly the topic of leadership. In this scenario the leader could be the sponsor or another senior person in the company – it doesn't really matter. What this individual must have is the vision and the drive to carry the team and maybe the company along on the journey. We all assume that this needs to be a main board director or VP, but as we discussed in Step 3 earlier in the book such people may not be best suited for the a task of this kind. It needs to be the *right* person not just *some* person.

These environmental factors are incredibly important to the success of any such initiative and they should be thought about before any activity is undertaken. One general approach is to have a plan in place for what to do when these sorts of things need to be done. I have seen companies that have created an Innovation plan to use when an idea or situation crops up : it lays out how things will happen and what resources will be available and when. Although this approach can work, my thoughts are that it is too prescriptive and sort of goes against the Innovation ethos. However as I have said so many times in the book, it is whatever works for you and your company.

Step 4. What are the barriers going to be?

Analysis of the questionnaire responses will give an indication of the barriers, and these results should be presented to the management team who participated in the workshop in Step 1. These results may come as a bit of a shock as it is unlikely that they will paint a rosy picture of the company – particularly its ability to Innovate. This can cause some negative feelings towards the initiative, but the results should be put in context by comparing the results to those of other internal teams and other external companies through the Innovation index.

Time for some more workshops. Ask the management team to nominate individuals who they think would benefit from being involved in the Innovation initiative or would add value to it. Bring these individuals together in groups of six to eight with instructions to paint the vision of the future and then present back their results. Having identified the barriers, work with the teams to establish what their priorities are and whether there are any others that should be considered.

There are a couple of techniques you could use in these workshops to look for ways to overcome the barriers. The first is the 'barrier boxes' technique, where the barrier is written on one side of a cardboard box and the boxes are built into a wall – the group members each take a box and write solutions to the barrier on the other five faces; the wall is then rebuilt with the best solutions facing forward. The second technique is roadmapping; in this type of workshop, the barriers are written either on cards or on a whiteboard, and linkages are drawn between any that have connections. These could be strategic goals, people, money, competition or any other factor that provides a connection. The group then discusses the linkages, aiming to reduce or minimise the barriers. Both of these techniques along with many others are described in greater detail in Appendix 4.

Step 5. The dance of Innovation

You will have already started this step when you sent out the Innovation audit questions. You will probably have created some intrigue within the community you have engaged with and there should be a buzz beginning.

The real power of this step is the empowerment it provides for people. There is no better way to change the culture of the company than by getting the people involved with the Innovation or strategic initiative. Their passion for their activity or initiatives will have an enabling effect on everyone they talk to – it will give them permission to do, think and act differently.

So how can you encourage this dance to take place? Well there are a couple of mechanisms that can be employed. The first is to actively promote the dance by briefing people involved that part of their role is to become advocates and evangelists for whatever the initiative is. It can be the most boring of process improvements, but if you talk about it with enthusiasm and passion it will be infectious. The second part of this active briefing is communication of the formal sort. If any workshops are run, make sure plenty of photographs are taken and put on a website or notice board somewhere where people will see them – make sure people know they are there. Offer to provide printouts or copies of the photographs for people to take home or pin up above their desks. Many participants will be proud of their involvement in the activity and will want to show people what they have been part of.

A second effect of these photos is the impact images have on the brain. Photographs and images of situations take people back to when the photo was taken – what it felt like, what was being said, even down to the detail of what they had eaten. The photographs tap into the right side of the brain, the creative and conceptual side, and trigger the recollection of many areas in a way that text doesn't – a diary doesn't evoke the same level of recall as a photo album for many people.

Step 6. Encourage break-out thinking

This is where the real challenge will begin. The first response to any initiative – particularly one that has the word Innovation in it – is: 'We've done this before' or 'It will never work' or 'How much is this going to cost?' I have heard them all before as well as probably a hundred others.

Our internal self-belief system – the things we have learned and the things we know – holds us back from thinking differently, particularly where experiences in the past that have been traumatic or negative inform our thinking when approaching the next situation. When approaching something we haven't experienced before we instinctively look for experiences in our past that are like the one we are currently facing. On many occasions we do not have a model to work from, and we then try and make one up for ourselves. Instinctively we make sure that we do not put ourselves in danger – either physical or social – and therefore we don't take risk. These thought processes use some of our lower brain functions and are linked to our 'fight or flight' response. Some can overcome the instinct for self-preservation and will throw themselves into danger to get the adrenalin hit – this is true just as easily for real-life danger as it is for apparent danger. When trying to get people to think differently these factors can seriously affect the success of any Innovative initiative.

So how can we overcome these restrictive thoughts? In this example of trying to get new business, the need to overcome 'stuck' thinking – thinking as we always have done – is incredibly important. I have run many workshops which have tried to solve this exact problem, and the biggest issue is how to stop people just coming up with the same old ideas, the same old 'chestnuts' which come out every time people are asked. So what would you do to get people to come up with new ideas?

There are a number of approaches that I would try to get people thinking differently. In this example it may be useful to look at other companies' business models to see if there are lessons that can be learned. To stimulate teams and individuals I have put together a list of companies with particular business models, which will hopefully draw out some radical thought. The companies I use are:

Company	Business model attributes
easyJet	Low cost no frills.
Nike	Superb marketing front end with outsourced manufacture.
McDonald's	Think local, act global: franchised dealership with power of centralised mass purchasing.
Amazon	Strong online brand coupled with low-cost products and cross selling.
Tesco	Strong customer focus, low prices and employee loyalty.

I get groups or individuals to look at their own company and analyse how one of these companies would enter its market: What would their strategy be, which customers would they target and why, how would they structure themselves to maximise their market share, and what would the press/media be saying? What could you learn from this exercise, what insights can you gain, how would you and your company respond?

A second approach would be to assume your company are to be or have been bought out by one of these companies. What would their strategies be, how would they change your product strategy, sourcing strategy, customer strategy and employee strategy? What insights can be drawn from this exercise?

The benefit of this approach is to force people to think differently – getting them to look at their own situation from a completely different angle.

A different, but equally effective approach is to use the 'other people's shoes' template in Appendix 4. This again gets people to look at their situation through other people's eyes, with different value sets and different needs/desires.

Step 7. Learn to notice things differently

As I have mentioned previously, I think this is one of the more fun steps in the 10-step Innovation process. In this scenario the first thing to do is to stand back and look at the situation through new eyes – see things differently. Start to ask the questions nobody thought of or were too afraid or embarrassed to ask. For most of our lives we learn to conform to what is expected; certainly when I was young, the wrong question or comment was often greeted with a quick crack round the ear. After a short while you learn that asking these questions or making these comments is painful!

In business life our conditioning continues as we learn what is acceptable and what is not – usually by observing others and the stories that are told around the company about what was done to somebody who asked the wrong question (this could almost be the subject of a book in its own right!).

I am always reminded when I go into corporate senior management meetings of the children's story of the emperor's new clothes – where nobody dares tell him he is naked when his tailors convince him that he is wearing clothes of magical qualities. Most people are so keen to fit into the company that they conform very quickly to what is expected, and therefore the questions that should be asked never are.

In our example of the competitor entering our marketplace, what questions should we actually ask? Well the obvious ones are about why you had to read in the *Sunday Times* that this was happening – about what had happened to your competitive intelligence system. The first thing I would want to know is how realistic the claims are – not that I wouldn't believe what I read in the press, but it has been known for companies to 'seed' stories to boost their share price.

But apart from the obvious, what are the awkward questions that should come out of this news? The key questions are about the company's ability to change and face up to the challenge or get out of the business.

What are our *actual costs* today? Interestingly many companies I have worked with do not have any definitive idea of the true cost base and rely on an 'ancient' business model to inform them. This means they are taking decisions that are based on some very suspect information sometimes. There are a few companies such as Tesco that do understand their costs to the penny, and these are the ones that are really pushing the envelope in terms of customer alignment – as their market position shows.

What is the *true profitability* of our products? Again this is something of a Holy Grail for many organisations. Do we go for a fully allocated cost model, which apportions central overheads into the figures, or a discrete cost model that just looks as the costs of delivering and servicing the particular product or service being offered? Accountants will argue both ways; my own thoughts are that a fully allocated cost gives a much more realistic view, but the product guys will argue strongly for a discrete costing model. The decision is yours at the end of the day.

What is the *true customer profitability*? How much do each of our customers spend and on what? This may sound a stupid question – but for many organisations, particularly the larger ones, this can be a nightmare as they may have different sales teams, a large multinational company may have several purchasing teams and there are many other complications. The usual response to this is that we need a new IT system that will give us a single view of the customer – *wrong answer*. This will take several years to implement, cost at least four times the original estimate, and probably be out of date by the time it is installed. I believe the answer is a people one: the challenge is to get people talking again and come out from behind their computer screens!

Step 8. Harvest ideas

One of the biggest frustrations for many people involved in Innovation and creativity is that many of the ideas are not actually new. In the Innovation Lab we generated over 168,000 ideas in the eight years I was involved in the facility. However, many of these ideas were quite similar; in fact if we distilled them down there were probably only 10–20 themes. The Innovation fund also generated many ideas; some of these were taken up, but in actuality only a very small percentage.

Most of the ideas or suggestions were rejected for one reason or another. Was it because they were bad ideas? No, it is just that the timing or the conditions were wrong.

So how do you harvest these ideas? How do you make sure that a little 'nugget' – the idea that could change the company – is not lurking in a report, spreadsheet or database somewhere. The easiest way is to get a small team of two or three people running every workshop that generates ideas in the company. When we first built the Innovation Lab I was that person. Because I was involved in all the workshops, I knew what had gone before and could build the linkages – as well as bringing to each session knowledge and insights from all the other others. A further advantage of this approach is that I became a 'hub' for knowledge within the company: I knew pretty much all that was going on, what all the strategies were, how the company and staff were reacting to situations and where the problems were. At the time I didn't realise what was happening and didn't maximise the knowledge and position I found myself in – looking back, I could have done so much more had I realised.

In reality however, this approach is not a viable solution for most companies; it is a luxury that cannot be afforded on a permanent basis. More typically, external facilitators or consultancies are used to run these workshops (which introduces a further complication as this knowledge can 'leak' out of the company and be lost, or at worst used by competitors).

So what other approaches are there? One of the most effective is to either build or buy an ideas management system – what used to be called a knowledge management system – where information is shared across the company. There are whole shelves of books on the subject of knowledge management so I don't intend to replicate their ideas in this book. What I will cover, however, is what needs to be contained in any ideas database/management system. The first thing is of course the idea itself. This should be as concise as possible without losing anything that would make it understandable in six or 12 months time.

It should also contain the details of where the idea comes from and who originated it, along with contact details – important if further clarification is needed. Information about why it wasn't used or acted upon at the time it was originated is also useful; these barriers may change in the future and it is possible to search a database for the ideas that may become viable if there are particular changes or conditions. The database should also contain information regarding the scale of the idea – either in terms of financial/ volumetric factors or of its potential impact on the company or individual. It is important that somebody 'owns' this database and cares about it enough to keep it up to date and relevant. However it should not become one of these things that grows its own organisation to support it. I have seen suggestion schemes and knowledge management systems spawn teams of 20 people to 'service' them; they attract critical attention when cost reductions and efficiencies are required, and they disappear into oblivion.

Step 9. Develop new ways of working

If you always do what you have always done, you will always get what you have always got.

This age-old saying, which doesn't seem to be attributed to anyone in particular, is very relevant when trying to undertake new Innovative activities and initiatives. Many teams have great ideas but fail when they get back into the office because they try and implement them in traditional ways. So many great ideas are 'squashed' by the use of traditional deployment techniques when people get back to the 'treacle' of the company. This is the wrong kind of sticky!

New ways of doing things should be found when trying to do new things. One approach is to use the model in the previous section by looking at how people in other companies have done things. However, this is not always the best approach as the conditions, culture and people in the other company will be different, and their ways may not work for you. What is important though is to look at what lessons can be learned from these companies – or more importantly many companies – as the more ideas you can get the better!

Another source is of course the media – whether this is the *Harvard Business Review* or the *Sun* (a UK Tabloid newspaper that has a downmarket reputation), it may give you ideas that you can use.

I have recently been involved in a series of workshops and initiatives using the GE Workout approach, which gets the people who are doing the job to find a way of making something happen in a short period of time – typically less than 90 days. This compressed deployment time forces people to think of new ways of doing things and new things to do! There are problems with this approach as people can tend to take short cuts, but that is sometimes a small price to pay for the benefit of just getting things done.

So in our example of trying to launch new products or services, reduce costs and retain customers, how can you get your initiatives underway? The first thing could be to understand your competitor's strategy – what they are doing differently to achieve their results.

One approach which is morally reprehensible but which I know does happen is to advertise a non-existent job at a higher salary than your competitor is paying. Chances are that people from the competitor will apply, and when you interview them you can find out a huge amount about their strategies (the candidate is then found to be unsuitable for the job and is not taken on). As the job never existed, some companies see this as a cheap way of getting a huge amount of competitive information. As I say, I in no way condone this but I do know it happens in a surprisingly large number of companies.

How can you get information honestly? Most companies like to get external publicity (we discussed its advantages earlier in this book) so one great tactic is a search of the media – particularly sector specific or IT publications – to find out what the competition is doing. Technology companies love to brag about the contracts they have won and the successes that have achieved, so finding out what equipment has been sold or what software has been installed may very well give you an insight into your competitor's strategy. There are a number of search services which offer access to this type of information over the web and a whole raft of consultancies who will do it for you – but don't forget you may lose intellectual capital if you go the latter route. Make sure you have a watertight contract or the consultant could go back to your competitor with information about your company! Not that I am paranoid but I have seen these things happen so many times.

Once you have the information you require about how your competitor is planning to achieve its objectives, then it is time to call a 'council of war': a workshop at this stage would probably be an excellent idea. In this situation you could pull together a team of around six or eight key people from around the company. These need not all be senior managers, and it probably better if they are not, but should be those who can make a difference in the company and are listened to – key influencers. At the workshop I would 'download' all the information and insights that have been found to the group and then split the them up to role-play the potential situations that might arise. I call this technique I call 'war-gaming', and it is detailed in Appendix 4 along with the appropriate template.

Out of these activities should come further insights into how you can compete or even collaborate, and the beginnings of a strategy for addressing the future. The strategy should have a driver and senior management sponsor whose job it is to clear the 'roadblocks' and problems for the driver, creating the environment for success. The sponsor and driver should meet frequently to pick up any problems before they become too big – but more importantly to build on any successes and make sure the 'dance' is done and done well.

Step 10. Benchmark and measure

No initiative would be complete without having appropriate and effective metrics in place – not only to measure the project or initiative itself but more importantly the success of the overall programme and therefore, you hope, ensure its success. Bearing in mind the old adage 'you are what you measure', it is important that the measures you put in place actually measure the things you want to achieve. For example if your measurements are all of the number of ideas generated, then you know that you are going to get loads and loads of ideas; whether any of them will turn into anything that the company can actually use is another question.

Similarly if the measure is taking ideas into action, then some idea *will* be taken into action whether it is any good or not! I have experienced both of these scenarios, and when you are 'in the thick of it' you don't see what is happening until it is too late.

In the 'big initiative' scenario we are considering here, a measure of success could be placed around market share, and there needs to be an agreed way of measuring it before you start. This is rather a long-term

measure, however, and if the idea is to do something within a short –
90 day – window then other alternatives should be sought. Maybe cost
reduction or increased efficiency could be a measure, or something as
simple as understanding the competitor better. Whatever is chosen
should encourage the behavioural change you are looking for as well
as positioning the company to achieve its particular goals.

It is essential to benchmark what you are doing if you are going to
gain credibility within the company, particularly with your peers and
sponsor. This can often be difficult as it is not always easy to find
companies that are doing what you are doing (if they were you probably wouldn't want to talk to them anyway as they might be your
competitors). Try to find similar activities in other sectors or market
segments, and companies that have undertaken similar initiatives –
typically the more prestigious the company the better.

One approach is to offer them access to information on your
initiatives as well as offering them mutual benchmarking of your
activities against theirs. If possible try to find a group of companies
that have been on the journey as this will provide a wealth of knowledge and help to stop you getting trapped. There are many organisations and associations that will provide either a benchmark or
benchmarking services, but my experience is that they will only
provide access to 'sterilised' information – interpreted rather than
'raw' data. This can be a hindrance as you are actually buying somebody's view, a perception, rather than reality.

Scenario II: changing the culture

It is Monday morning on a warm spring day in May. The CEO has been
away for a couple of weeks on vacation in the Maldives and has had time
to think about the direction of the company. He has been reading the
latest best-selling business book by Howard Wright (OK, I can dream
can't I?) which talks about turning the company round by bringing
FUN (which stands for '*Finding your Unifying Network*') into the work-
place. (This is of course a fictitious initiative and is used for illustrative
purposes only at this stage – though there may just be something in it.)

He has decided that this is the thing that is going to solve all the
company's problems – whatever they are. Yes, I know you have heard

this before; however, it will provide support for some of your initiatives that you hope will change the company for the good, so adapt the scenario for your own needs.

Step 1. Understand the destination

In this scenario this is probably going to be the hardest step of all, because the CEO probably doesn't know what he is trying to achieve other than to 'turn the company round' and 'create a sense of success' or whatever the latest buzz phrases are. However, if you don't get this step right you are doomed to failure – whatever you do won't be right and if you're not careful it could become seriously career limiting.

I once worked for a marketing manager who was known as a bit of a tyrant. He would send people off on a project for some new product or service; when they came back with their proposals he typically hated the ideas and sent them away to get it right next time. On one occasion I spent three days with him at a visioning workshop and he casually mentioned that he loved computer games – particularly the Dungeons and Dragons type where someone is in distress and your role is to fight the dragons and collect the keys and other tools that will open the doors and let you through to the princess or the treasure.

What I realised was that he was playing his role as marketing director in the same way he was role-playing in the virtual world. He knew he had a quest: to launch a new product or something. He sent his team off to get the keys to the doors or the magic bucket. When they came back he realised that he didn't have the right things to get him to the next stage, so he sent them off again. To them he seemed to be indecisive, but he was just trying to get to the next stage of the game.

The insight that this brought me changed the way I approach any discussion with or presentation to him. I knew what I had to do – rather than the answer, what he needed was the thing to take him to the next stage. When I tell people this story, particularly those who knew him, I get some very strange looks. However, I was the one who seemed to succeed as he usually accepted what was said and built on the conversation or presentation rather than rubbishing it.

What does this have to do with our quest for FUN? Well in this scenario, rather than try and understand the destination by quizzing the CEO and his team – who probably wouldn't know anyway – my strategy would be to bring a few scenarios to him and a set of tools and techniques that would let him better understand not only the destination but more importantly how he would know when they got there.

Very often senior managers have got to their position not because they have the ability to develop visions but because of their ability to manage the company closely on a day-to-day basis. Asking for a vision or a scenario from these people can be very problematic. What you usually get is a plan that works from today forward – 2 per cent growth based on GDP, 3.7 per cent or whatever. Although this approach is OK for day-to-day management and is vital for organisational success, it may not be appropriate for developing alternative futures. This is why the best approach with this type of managers may be to give them some scenarios which they can then choose from – avoiding the embarrassment of not being able to create them themselves.

Step 2. Understand where you are

How aligned to the new vision is the company today? There is no point in setting up a whole new set of initiatives with staff who have also probably seen it all before, if all that is needed is a slight tweak here and there.

So how do you understand your current position? Well hopefully the first step will have revealed a set of characteristics, values and other cultural elements that the new organisation will have, so this will be your starting point. How are you measuring up today to these new characteristics? How far are your values different from those that are desired? There are several ways you can find out; clearly you can undertake the Innovation audit, although you would need to modify it slightly to find out your particular needs.

A second approach would be to interface with the staff – OK, just talk to them! This can be done via focus groups or Internet blogs; one company, quite inventively, used a graffiti board where staff could write down what they thought. This latter solution is probably the best way to find out what is actually happening within the company, although it may not be what you want to hear. If you do adopt this approach it is good to write specific questions on the board as you are more likely to get the sort of comments you're interested in rather than just a list of whinges.

Step 3. Create the right environment

As I have mentioned many times before in this book, having the right environment and resources is key to the success of any initiative. In this scenario, where the company is looking for major culture change in a relatively short time, the temptation is to throw money at the initiative to make sure it works and sticks. The risk in this approach is that it becomes another white elephant and is seen by everybody – the board, the senior managers and the staff – as a total waste of time and money.

When money is thrown at a project, it is usually spent on consultants. In that case, the company is passing responsibility to somebody else to make the initiative happen and trying to avoid any blame if it fails. Unfortunately consultants often have a different set of priorities and values, which seem to be based on making the contract last as long as they can and getting knowledge and information out of the company which they can use elsewhere. This is a very cynical view I know, but again I have seen this so many times. It is in their interest to keep things going for as long as possible, or if there is a fixed-price contract make it so tight that any slight deviation is a chargeable event.

So what is the right environment for a culture change initiative such as this? Firstly there needs to be a good solid vision of what the company is trying to achieve by going down this road. This should be articulated in such away that everyone in the company can understand and buy in to it – from the frontline staff to the senior managers and the catering and cleaning staff. The simpler the vision is the better, so that people can remember it.

When writing a vision, *do not try to write a vision statement with a group.* (Groups are great for many things, but writing collectively is not one of them!) Ask one or two people to try drafting a vision statement based on the group's discussion, bring it back to the group, and revise it until you have something that your members can agree on and that your leaders share with enthusiasm.

Vision is defined in one dictionary as: 'An image of the future we seek to create'. A vision statement describes in graphic terms where the goal-setters want to see themselves in the future. It may describe how they see events unfolding over 10 or 20 years if everything goes exactly as hoped.

Things that kill a good vision are:

- tradition
- fear of ridicule
- stereotypes of people, conditions, roles and management teams
- complacency of some stakeholders
- fatigued leaders
- short-term thinking
- 'naysayers'.

The characteristics of an excellent vision statement are:

- clarity and absence of ambiguity
- a vivid, clear and unambiguous picture
- the image of a bright future (hope)
- memorable and engaging expression
- realistic, achievable aspirations
- rational alignment with organisational values and culture
- time limits for achieving any goal or objective.

A vision statement should not be confused with a mission statement. The dictionary defines mission as: 'purpose, reason for being'.

So what about this 'right environment'? We have talked about leadership and the importance of vision: there needs to be management buy-in to the direction the company is going. Managers need to create an environment that will allow the staff to think and act differently, and the necessary reward and recognition structures need to be in place to support and encourage the right behaviours.

Step 4. What are the barriers going to be?

In this scenario, identifying the barriers will probably be the easiest step to undertake, as many people will know what is most likely to stop this initiative happening. The likelihood is that there have been similar initiatives in the past, and there will be people who bear battle scars from these and are more than willing to tell you what all the problems will be. Be cautious though, as their views will be coloured by their personal experiences. Take on board their comments but don't take them as gospel; see them as a component of the problems rather than the whole problem.

Are there new people in the company – people who have been there for less than six months – who can give you some insights? These people may well have experience from other companies or situations and will certainly give you a different perspective on the possible barriers.

Other sources are customers: ask them what they think would stop whatever it is. You may be surprised at how much they know about your organisation and the way it works – or more importantly, doesn't work. One by-product of this is that it may forge a stronger relationship with them, as they will feel valued and important.

Lastly what about the press? What are they saying about your company and your competitors? There is an interesting technique I picked up from a US consultancy that was expert in bibliographic analysis – counting the times certain words appear in the press and their relationship to each other.

When I first saw the technique I was very sceptical, but after a couple of passes through their systems I actually found it very enlightening. The technique is based on identifying a key set of words that will define the new company and the market segment you are in. Typically this will be somewhere around 10–20 words. By searching for these words and their position in media articles, you can assess how important they are – people are or are not talking about them – and how they are being used in the media.

So for example if 'fun' was one of the words and 'customer' was another, you would search for these words either in a simple Google search of the news or through a subscription to a media cataloguing service such as LexisNexis (www.lexisNexis.com). These services allow complex searches to be undertaken very rapidly in either specific or general segments of publications.

In our example, if there are lots of references to the two words then it is probably too late to try to brand yourself as a 'FUN' company; if there were very few references, however, it could be that you would steal a march on your competitors. The searching can be further refined by market segment, industry and of course other words. This technique may not be suitable for your initiative, but on the times I have tried it for other companies the insights have been significant and have led to some major new strategies being developed.

So you have found that there is some major cultural and organisational change to do, there are not many references to the things you want to do in the press and therefore you will probably become a market leader in this initiative, and the staff don't seem too hostile to the ideas – what do you do next?

Step 5. The dance of Innovation

The dance should have already started when you began talking to the staff to find out where you are today. The secret is to understand that the dance is happening and to manage it proactively. One of the most significant problems that you will face is cynicism from the staff, particularly if you are in an organisation where the 'magic bullet' project or initiative is the norm – one where there is always the next big thing that will solve all the company's problems.

So how do you overcome this scepticism and cynicism? I have found an effective way is to get frontline people actively involved and let them tell their stories – through presentations, videos or articles in the internal magazines. This is the true dance of Innovation as it gives people permission to do things differently themselves and join in the dance, which hopefully creates viral Innovation – self-sustaining change. Although this is great in theory I have not actually experienced this Innovation 'fusion', as typically what happens is that the corporate immune system closes round the initiative or people to stop disruptive change taking place.

Using 'real people', frontline staff, gives their colleagues someone they can identify with, and as long as the 'establishment' does not script the communication the effect can be electric. Hearing one of your friends or colleagues enthuse about an initiative or project is much more powerful than reading about it in the company magazine or receiving an email.

Another way of starting or encouraging the dance is to get publicity in the external press. A positive case study or review in the media has an amazing effect on the internal audience – the pride effect clicks in. I was in a restaurant a couple of weeks ago and on the next table was a group of friends who had obviously worked together sometime in the past. One of the group was enthusing about a project and about how great it was to be part of the company, while another was rubbishing the activity and the company. The enthusiast then said that there had been an article in some seemingly obscure industry publication, and the other guy's attitude changed immediately. The fact that something had been published about the initiative seem to say it was OK and therefore the company must be OK.

The question is how to get people to be enthusiastic about whatever you are trying to achieve so they become advocates and almost evangelists for it. One of the companies I worked for decided that it wanted to achieve this sense of pride, and announced that it was going to be a 'great place to work'. A large amount of money was spent on publicising the initiative, and objectives and targets started to be put in place. It almost became part of the bonus scheme that individuals had to say that it was a 'great place to work'.

The employee satisfaction survey had a whole section on the topic, and managers were targeted with significantly improving the scores (when the initiative started less than 20 per cent of the employees felt it was a 'great place to work' – at the end it went up to 30 per cent I believe). The initiative is probably still going on and money is being invested, but being told to say the words doesn't make it so. How many of the company's employees would sit in the pub or restaurant and say 'you know, my company is a great place to work'? I guess not many. For me, the big stick approach is a sign of helplessness in the management. They don't know how to do something so the easiest way is to mandate it.

People need to respect the management and the company, to understand the company values and believe in what is trying to be achieved. This cannot be mandated and must be built in a structured and appropriate way – as part of an overall plan or strategy.

Step 6. Encourage break-out thinking

So we have out vision, our new values created in Step 1 of this example, and we understand where we are now and where we need to get to. But what has break-out thinking got to do with culture change?

I go back to a statement I highlighted earlier in the book: 'If you always do what you have always done, you will always get what you have always got.' If we carry on acting and behaving in the same old ways – even if we have some blindingly good vision and values set – nothing will change, believe me. You need to encourage different behaviour from everyone in the company, not just in specific situations but every day and in every way.

This can range from something as simple as encouraging casual dress in the office through to instigating team meetings to look at how the new vision could be implemented. Whatever approach you take, it needs to be taken seriously by everybody in the company from the CEO right down to the front line if it is going to be effective. It is also something that should be entered into for the long haul. Too many initiatives are started and never carried through to the point where true value is seen. The 'magic bullet' syndrome has much to answer for!

Look to encourage new and radical ideas on how the new vision or strategies could be encouraged and implemented within the company. Find a way of capturing these ideas and harvesting them to find the best. Although the easiest method is a suggestion scheme, that can prove to be unwieldy and ineffective in the long term. One major problem is the sheer volume of ideas that can be generated. I know of one scheme that had a very attractive reward attached to it that generated over 100,000 ideas in its first month. How on earth you could find the 'golden nugget' in that volume it is impossible to imagine. Moreover, such schemes can weaken morale. If an idea is rejected, the person who suggested it may feel offended and will probably not put another one forward.

So the question is how else you could gather people's ideas. The answer is 'break-out thinking': think radically about how you can get the really great ideas out. There are a number of approaches you could take, from traditional to radical break-out thinking. On the traditional front, one approach would be to use something like the Workout methodology pioneered by Jack Welsh in GE in the 1980s, but with modifications. Rather than taking the unnecessary work out of someone's job, which is the whole purpose of the process, get people to think about how they could 'live the vision': what they could do in 90 days or less to encourage people to think and act differently. Get them to 'sell' it to the senior management, and then empower them to go and do it with whatever support structures and resources are appropriate.

A different approach would be to set up a competition that encouraged staff to create something that told *their* story of life in the new company and how they got there. You could use different media – text, video, photos, Internet and so on – and you will be surprised how inventive people can be. The material can then be distributed through the company and people can vote on their favourite approach or the one that they think would be the most effective. This ties very much in with the storytelling approach that is covered in Appendix 3 of this book. The research indicates that this approach has the most stickiness and will produce memorable output if nothing else.

A third approach – and definitely more radical – is to invite outsiders in to help define a strategy. By outsiders I don't mean consultants but schoolchildren, students, ex-employees, even old-age pensioners. All will have some knowledge or skill that may be able to help build the culture change vehicle.

Step 7. Learn to notice things differently

We all walk around every day with blinkers on – or so it seems. We are conditioned to see what we want to see and not what is actually there. We tend not to notice the odd or the strange but rather to somehow tune it out, almost as if we feared it would be too difficult to deal with. This ability to filter out the unwanted is a valuable capability when facing some adversities, but when trying to implement change it can be a huge hindrance.

This step of the process is about noticing things that we don't normally see, celebrating behaviour changes however small they are, and reinforcing the vision. Most UK organisations spurn failure – the offender is pilloried or even dismissed – whereas other cultures seem to celebrate it as a chance for the individual involved to learn a valuable lesson.

The question, then, is how you can encourage everyone to notice things differently – particularly when *all* you are trying to change is people's behaviour. Positive feedback is one answer which should be encouraged right through the company. This is the one step that can be effected from the top down as well as from the bottom up; getting the CEO to positively acknowledge people's change in behaviour and action can have a huge effect on the initiative. However peer and colleague feedback is also powerful, although criticism can be taken the wrong way if you are not careful and this approach should not be overused. The 'have a nice day' approach to feedback – that every time you meet someone you tell them how wonderful they are – can become ineffective very quickly.

Step 8. Harvest ideas

I have touched on this earlier in Step 6 on 'Encourage break-out thinking', where mechanisms such as suggestion schemes were discussed. Although stimulating ideas can be relatively easy, picking the ones that you want to do something with and that will have a positive impact on your initiative is more difficult.

As discussed earlier in the book, finding the idea swarms is the key. Do you have loads of ideas on a particular subject or topic? What are the common themes? Can the ideas be grouped or clustered to reflect the vision in some way? If they can, then either do this on an Excel spreadsheet or, if there are not that many, write them on index cards and stick them to the wall using Blu-Tack.

Then stand back. The human brain is great at recognising patterns, whether these are in information or in the physical world. Take some time out just to stare at them – don't try to re-arrange them at this stage. Then walk away. Take some time out, and your brain will be subconsciously processing the ideas/cards in the background, and you will find that when you go back to them in 10–15 minutes the patterns will be obvious. The relationships and linkages will just jump out at you. If you were to actively work on them you usually wouldn't get the same result, as the brain has not had time to process the information and patterns sufficiently. Then what you get is a 'knee jerk' decision or direction.

Theoretically women should be better at spotting these patterns than men. In the book *Why Men Don't Listen and Women Can't Read Maps*, Allan and Barbara Pease put forward the theory that women have a wider peripheral view than men. I believe the figures are a 65 per cent field of view for women and an 18 per cent field of view for men. The theory suggests this is due to their different roles in prehistoric times, when women acted as carers for children and men as hunters. Whether you believe it or not, it is a good excuse for us men not being able to find anything in the fridge! I must admit I haven't yet done the research to support this theory, but it is now on my list and no doubt I will include the results in the next book.

Once the patterns are obvious and the linkages start to form, then look for the characteristics of the ideas – their DNA if you like. There will be things that are common to a group of cards or ideas, and there will be things that are different. Take the common elements as a given and concentrate on the differences. This is where the wow factor will probably be hiding. At this stage don't dismiss anything. Don't forget there are no bad ideas – just ideas at the wrong time or ones that need the other things or conditions to be in place.

Step 9. Develop new ways of working

In this scenario, the aim of this step is to encourage new behaviour in the company that aligns with the vision. It sounds simple when you say it like that, but in reality it is probably the hardest step to achieve effectively.

There have been numerous books and theories which talk about 'walking the talk' and 'management by walking around'. At the time these ideas were developed they were exactly what was required as organisations came out of a bureaucratic, hierarchical state, and although I am not sure I still agree with all they were pushing, at least they got managers talking to staff. In some cases, at least. I had a recent experience in the UK Civil Service where a senior manager was asked to pose for an internal magazine with some new staff at a refurbished building and have a chat with them – he responded that he didn't talk to staff only to managers! It's hard to believe that this attitude still exists today, but in 2006 I can assure you it does!

Step 10. Benchmark and measure

Last but by no means least is the benchmark and measure step. This is the one I find the hardest but the most rewarding at the same time. Why is it the hardest? Because you are trying to measure something intangible – a feeling, an emotion, a behaviour change. In an individual this is possible though the use of one of the many psychometric tests available. In an organisation, however, it is a different story.

In one of my jobs I suggested to the MD that a good way of understanding the 'state' of the company was to measure the number of illicit affairs that were taking place. This was based on the idea that if people were happy in their job and felt relaxed they were more likely to have an affair. I realise that this is not a politically correct approach and it didn't go down too well at the time. The thought that this could become a bonus-worthy target could land the company in hot water in the courts with disgruntled partners. The other question is how would you measure it, and more interestingly how would you report it in the annual report and accounts?

Although the 'affair' idea may not have been one of my best, it is important that you think differently when trying to measure the culture change within the company. Traditional measures may not be appropriate, and very often staff will use any questionnaire either to vent their anger or to tell you what you want to hear – 'you are what you measure' after all. So how else could you tell if the changes that you had initiated had had the effect you were looking for.

The ubiquitous staff survey will of course provide an indication, as would the 'exit survey' approach used by some retail supermarkets that interview staff when they leave the company. This approach should be used with care as staff can find it intimidating and the couple of times I have used it I found a high degree of suspicion and reticence. There are a number of survey tools available on the Internet and many of these are available free of charge, although there may be restrictions on the number of people who can be surveyed or the number of questions you can ask. A quick search on Google should provide a list of suitable websites.

One brave technology company installed a graffiti wall in the restaurant at their head office. Staff were encouraged to write up the things that they thought were good and the gripes they had. Although the initial response was just to write down all the problems, after a couple of weeks people started to write up positive statements as well as negative ones, and after about six weeks over 90 per cent of the statements were positive.

A culture change initiative had been running in parallel with the graffiti wall, and the management took the change from negative to positive as an indication of the change in staff attitude generally. Although there seemed to be a correlation it was never proved, and in fact the negative comments returned after a couple of months and the graffiti wall was finally taken down and replaced with a nice picture. I believe the company had tried something very important – to get unadulterated views from its staff – but as it failed to act on the responses, both the positive and the negative, it had devalued this great idea.

Chapter 14

Where next: what is the next step or indeed the next journey?

If we look at the history of Innovation, since its inception in the early 1930s the concept has gone through a range of models – each reflecting environmental and local changes. Various 'drivers' or levers that have been prevalent at the time have also driven them. In the case of the UK, these changed as society changed. In the 1970s it was science that was driving Innovation and invention. In the 1990s connectivity was the driving force with the advent of the Internet and the World Wide Web. Today in the early 2000s we have entered a new phase that is an extension from the network model and is based on collaboration. In the future I predict that the next phase or model will be built on social Innovation, with many more people being involved in a company's Innovation and change activities than has ever been seen before.

So what is social Innovation and why is it important? The traditional process-driven frameworks that we have seen in Innovation over the last 60 years are becoming too restrictive. This, coupled with the connectivity offered by today's technologies, will allow companies as well as individuals to engage in Innovation activity on a scale that has no precedent. The ability to engage with a wide and diverse group of people will bring new opportunities to quickly and effectively tailor product, services and styles to meet local and national needs.

In this context the nature of Innovation itself changes, and the issues raised by this new way of 'being' will bring challenges as yet unforeseen. If customers, employees and potential competitors/ collaborators are actively involved in the Innovation process, then this will change the dynamics of the company – as well as the culture itself. Innovation is set to become a normal way of working if companies embrace these changes and are open to new ways of working and engagement at all levels.

So what will social Innovation look and feel like in the real world? What will be different, how will it be viewed? In some small areas we are already seeing social Innovation in action – particularly in the mobile phone market.

People are 'tailoring' and personalising their phones to their own needs and desires. Companies such as Nokia are picking up on these subtle changes and incorporating them into their manufacturing lines. This has led to new designs, new styles and new ways of using the software – and most of these changes have been driven by the customer, not by some R&D department in a room back at head office. Although Nokia currently tends to work with a small number of the customers, this could just as easily be millions if the technology and mindset are there to support them. With a short product lifecycle in the mobile phone market, around five months, this kind of change is relatively easy. However for many companies the ability to react quickly to market needs is still seen as the Holy Grail.

One as yet unanswered question is: How does Innovation change in a truly open, global economy and marketplace? Are some countries more open to this new way of working than others? Are some countries better positioned to meet the challenges and needs of this new Innovation culture? Are there national characteristics and styles that are more effective when Innovation becomes truly socialised?

The concept of social Innovation will have no boundaries and will be self-sustaining if it becomes a reality. Can companies, and more importantly governments, actively support the changes required to make this a reality?

The need to create the right environment is taken to a new level when social Innovation is occurring on a national and/or global scale. I have talked at length in this book about the factors that go into creating the right environment in companies' Innovation activities and initiatives as well as at a personal level. These factors will be magnified many-fold when looked at on a national or global scale.

Is the 10-step approach still valid? I would argue that the approach is scalable to a national if not global level and many of the steps are still useable – maybe with some minor changes. In Step 1, the need to understand how society will change when it is fully engaged with the companies and agencies that provide products, services and infrastructure is still vital to any initiative – large or small.

In Step 2, understanding where society is today in terms of this new type of engagement is essential, as are the resources and environment needed to foster the new way of living and working. To gauge the success of any such initiative, benchmarking and measuring – particularly in a global context – will be vital to steer the necessary resources into the right areas. The concept, if not the reality, of the Innovation index is also still important.

Clearly, creating the right environment as described in Step 3 will be vital to the success of national and global innovation. Leadership will be an important factor, with the country's leaders or political parties providing a compelling strategic vision which can be understood and bought into by the populace. Effective funding models and access to support resources will be essential – and interestingly, providing these will be among the more difficult challenges leaders will face.

Although funding itself will probably not be a challenge, as the amounts required to make social innovation a reality are not huge in government terms, ensuring its effective use and measuring the impact/success of any investment will be important to maintain stakeholders' and society's confidence in the initiative. Government-funded initiatives are often seen as 'white elephants', with vast amounts of cash being ploughed into initiatives that never come to fruition, or if they do have dubious value – other than lining consultants' pockets!

The barriers outlined in Step 4 will of course be much larger – particularly when working on a national or global scale. However, the resources that are available to solve some of the these problems are also greater than those of a company or individual. As we live in an increasingly multicultural world there will be additional dimensions to be considered, as there will be different values, beliefs and cultural norms at play.

In Step 5 the dance of Innovation will be generated not through the traditional channels but more through the national media – a luxury companies and individuals don't have.

The other steps still appear to be valid, although less important when looking at the big picture on a national or global basis.

Another strand of Innovation for the future is the physical/virtual 'environment'. I have argued long and hard for the need for a physical environment – a place – where people can Innovate and think differently. I have been fortunate in that I have been involved in many such facilities. With the advent of new and exciting web environments, increased processing power, and improved storage and bandwidth, however, new possibilities must be opening up. The ability to create online Innovation labs is becoming a reality as the historic difficulties of providing fast and flexible infrastructures on which to build them are reducing on a daily if not hourly basis.

We have undertaken some experiments by addressing the same question or challenge in a physical Innovation environment (same time, same place) and also using the anonymous brainstorming software online (different time, different place). The results were interesting. People who were in the physical environment were a lot more creative – building on other people's ideas and thoughts – and the results were markedly better than using the same approach in a virtual environment. There was something very powerful about the social interaction that took place in the physical environment when compared with the brainstorming and categorising software of an online environment. This led us to try and understand the 'DNA' of the physical space. What was it about it that encouraged 'better' results? The rationale for this study was that if we could find out what it was that made the same-time/same-place situation better than the different-time/different-place one, then we might be able to take some of the characteristics of the former into the online world.

The only characteristic that seemed to be missing was the direct contact between people. Many of my interactions and interventions in Innovation have been at a 'people' level in face-to-face situations. Moving online removes the ability to see the 'whites of people's eyes' – seeing and sensing the group and how it is reacting to the situation, and so altering my behaviour and activity to match their mood.

The US navy has tried building online creativity rooms using avatars (virtual representations of individuals in a virtual world) to represent people attending the session, and colours or other symbols to represent the moods of the participants. However, this is very much dependent on the participants typing in how they feel, which somehow defeats the object. Maybe some human–machine link based on stress or skin resistance could be linked to a system to represent feelings. I am sure that there is a whole research topic on this; if there isn't, there soon will be. The navy project was successful at one level: they managed to create a multi-room meeting and creativity environment. The avatars did not really work however, as people didn't take the thing seriously; there is a fine line between fact and fiction in an online environment.

Clearly by the time this book is published some of these issues may have been addressed. Although I am still a firm believer in the face-to-face model of the physical environment, I look forward to being proved wrong!

The final challenge

The last topic in this chapter is a challenge. The word Innovation has lost its potency and in some cases its meaning in the modern age. It has become a 'catch-all' for anything that is slightly different or sometimes even the same. The words have become over-used and tired. As I mentioned in the first chapter of this book, the word 'innovation' is in nearly every report and set of accounts, most business plans and product advertisements. It's true meaning has somehow become lost in its over-use. So to the challenge: we need a new language for Innovation. We need some new words and phrases that will excite and enthuse people again – a new language for change.

On a personal note: where is my journey taking me next?

I have decided to try to make it in the 'real world' – that is, the world outside corporate structures. An opportunity to leave my previous role with a small voluntary redundancy package gave me the boost I needed to try something new. I have been fascinated how work just keeps turning up when you least expect it. I now have an income three times that of my last job, only work three days a week, am writing this book and have just secured an interim management job in the USA for two or three weeks a month.

For me the challenge was to describe my own future – what I wanted to achieve – and to look at where I was and what resources I had.

So things have changed. I took my own medicine and decided to take the 10 steps myself. And the future – well, I have no idea and it is wonderful and so exciting.

APPENDICES

Appendix 1

Innovation audit

Audit questionnaire

The following is a list of questions I used to audit the company's Innovation capability in 2000. The questions are grouped into three sections – looking at Innovation from an organisational perspective, a team or group perspective within the organisation, and from an individual's perspective. Each of these three can be used discretely, but the real power of the survey comes when all three are undertaken across a wide audience.

In each of the questions rank your agreement or disagreement on the scale 1–10. Ten means you agree completely with the statement and one that you are flatly disagreeing.

Organisational level

	Question	Response
1	Innovation in my role is critical to the success of the company	10 – – – – – – – 1
2	Everybody in the company is encouraged to share new ideas	10 – – – – – – – 1
3	There is a market demand for Innovation within our company	10 – – – – – – – 1
4	The physical environment within the company is not supportive of Innovation	10 – – – – – – – 1
5	Innovation and creativity are supported by the appraisal and objective-setting processes within the company	10 – – – – – – – 1
6	The company values Innovative and creative people	10 – – – – – – – 1
7	There is active discouragement of cross-functional contacts	10 – – – – – – – 1
8	The company actively celebrates success	10 – – – – – – – 1
9	There is an atmosphere of clock-watching in the company	10 – – – – – – – 1
10	If I have a great idea there are resources readily available to support me	10 – – – – – – – 1
11	There is an absence of formal management structures within my company	10 – – – – – – – 1
12	In order to survive the company has to Innovate	10 – – – – – – – 1
13	The company encourages colleagues to give me practical ideas to improve my work	10 – – – – – – – 1
14	Adaptable and creative people are valued by this company	10 – – – – – – – 1
15	New people starting are encouraged to be Innovative and creative	10 – – – – – – – 1
16	I would find presenting a new idea to senior management personally threatening	10 – – – – – – – 1
17	Asking for help from a work colleague is like asking a friend	10 – – – – – – – 1
18	Objectives and targets are set to encourage Innovation and creativity	10 – – – – – – – 1
19	There is a clear communication flow from senior management	10 – – – – – – – 1
20	As long as idea works, no one cares or minds where it comes from	10 – – – – – – – 1

Individual level

	Question	Response
1	I have a strong belief in my competence	10 – – – – – – 1
2	I tackle my work methodically	10 – – – – – – 1
3	If people disapprove of my work it does not bother me	10 – – – – – – 1
4	It is better to ask for forgiveness than permission	10 – – – – – – 1
5	I would rather use traditional ideas than dream up new ones	10 – – – – – – 1
6	I like to get positive feedback if have a new idea	10 – – – – – – 1
7	I like to evaluate an idea before putting it into practice	10 – – – – – – 1
8	My job requires me to be innovative	10 – – – – – – 1
9	I like to have frequent changes in the work that I do	10 – – – – – – 1
10	I am effective in generating and implementing new ideas	10 – – – – – – 1
11	I like to tackle problems one at a time	10 – – – – – – 1
12	The culture of the company constrains Innovation	10 – – – – – – 1
13	Shifting work goals make my job difficult	10 – – – – – – 1
14	I could achieve anything if I set my mind to it	10 – – – – – – 1
15	Making a difference in this company is really difficult	10 – – – – – – 1
16	I am seen as a non-conformist by my colleagues	10 – – – – – – 1
17	Time spent thinking up new ideas is time wasted	10 – – – – – – 1
18	I find it difficult to find a new perspective on old work problems	10 – – – – – – 1
19	I prefer to adapt traditional methods than think up new ones	10 – – – – – – 1
20	I really enjoy working in this company	10 – – – – – – 1

Team level

	Question	Response
1	My colleagues are very supportive when I have a good idea	10 – – – – – – – 1
2	My manager often puts obstacles in my way when developing new ideas	10 – – – – – – – 1
3	My colleagues are difficult to talk to about new ideas	10 – – – – – – – 1
4	My team is really good to work in	10 – – – – – – – 1
5	My manager is willing to take risks when implementing a new idea	10 – – – – – – – 1
6	We have fun in the team	10 – – – – – – – 1
7	Team meetings are often boring	10 – – – – – – – 1
8	I understand how the work my team does fits into the goals of the company	10 – – – – – – – 1
9	We have regular team briefings/meetings	10 – – – – – – – 1
10	My manager does not see work as a fun place	10 – – – – – – – 1
11	My team shows no enthusiasm for Innovation	10 – – – – – – – 1
12	I feel I can trust my colleagues to support any new idea I have	10 – – – – – – – 1
13	There is good communication between teams in this company	10 – – – – – – – 1
14	We regularly have team social events	10 – – – – – – – 1
15	My manager has both the ability and commitment to deliver the company vision	10 – – – – – – – 1
16	I feel proud of my team and what it has achieved	10 – – – – – – – 1
17	The team feels a sense of ownership of the corporate vision	10 – – – – – – – 1
18	I have respect for my colleagues in the team	10 – – – – – – – 1
19	The team works together to solve problems and resolve issues	10 – – – – – – – 1
20	I wish my colleagues would stop interrupting me and let me get on	10 – – – – – – – 1

Appendix 2

Innovation labs

Royal Mail Innovation Lab
Innovation Lab,
Coton House Learning and
Development Centre,
Rugby,
Warwickshire,
CV23 0AA

Phone: +44(0)1788 512179
Email: thelab@royalmail.com

University of Essex Innovation Labs
i-Lab,
Business Development Centre,
University of Essex Southend,
Princess Caroline House,
1 High Street,
Southend-on-Sea,
Essex,
SS1 1JE

Phone: +44(0)1702 238636
Email: bdc@essex.ac.uk

Southend i-Lab
Learning Partnerships,
Constable Building,
Wivenhoe Park,
Colchester,
CO4 3SQ

Phone +44(0)1206 87 3163
Email: ilabmanager@essex.ac.uk

University of East Anglia ILab
The Hub,
University of East Anglia,
Norwich,
NR4 7TJ

Phone: +44(0)1603 593483
Email: larc@uea.ac.uk

Reading University
Innovation Works,
Research and Enterprise Services,
Whiteknights House,
Whiteknights,
Reading,
RG6 6AH

Phone: +44(0)118 3786161
Email: innovationworks@reading.ac.uk

Hassenbrook College
iLab,
Hassenbrook School,
Hassenbrook Road,
Stanford-Le-Hope,
Essex,
SS17 7HD

Phone: +44(0)1375 665752
Email: i-lab@hassenbrook.org.uk

UK Government DTI Future Focus
Future Focus@dti,
UG72,
1 Victoria Street,
London,
SW1H 0ET

Phone: +44(0)20 7215 0299
Email: futurefocus@dti.gsi.gov.uk

Coventry University
The TechnoCentre,
Coventry University Technology Park,
Puma Way,
Coventry,
CV1 2TT

Phone: +44(0)24 7623 6023
Email:
creativitylab@cad.coventry.ac.uk

Appendix 3

Are you sitting comfortably?

The art of storytelling has been with us almost since the dawn of speech, with civilisations using stories and legends to pass on their history and culture. There are many examples of the power of stories that can be taken from history; these can be both positive and negative in nature.

Organisations use similar methods to pass on the culture of the company, using stories about people, projects and teams. These stories form the culture of the organisation – setting the rules, showing what is acceptable, reinforcing beliefs and so on. People joining the company bring their own stories, and these become part of the new corporate storybook.

The human brain is wired to work with patterns of information and variations in patterns. Humans make good use of the narrative pattern in stories. We engage with them, relate them to previous stories we have heard, remember them easily and retell them when appropriate. Stories speak to both parts of the human mind – its reason and its emotion. Stories provide a tool for articulating and focusing vision. They provide a medium of communication, both internally within an organisation and externally to customers, potential customers, business partners, rivals, investors and others.

Each of us understands things in at least two ways. First, we hear or read what is in front of us. For example at a presentation we read the slides and listen to the speaker. Second and more importantly, a little voice inside our heads tries to interpret what we are hearing and seeing, and to make it relevant for us, for our situation. Using stories provides a short-cut through these activities as the storyteller is doing some of the interpretation for the listener/reader. If you watch effective presenters and leaders, they use anecdotes and stories to illustrate points in their presentation. Interestingly, these stories are the things that people remember after the presentation, not the content of the slides. This is particularly true some weeks after the presentation.

The other issue around presentations and reports is that, if left to its own devices, the 'inner-voice' interprets the information in its own way – based on experiences, knowledge and prejudices and beliefs. If 20 people listen to the same presentation, there will be 20 different interpretations of what was said. Moreover, the information retained by these people is typically short lived. Most people cannot remember the details of a presentation 24 hours after the event. If the same information is presented as a story, everybody gets the same picture and a shared understanding is quickly arrived at. Research at the Royal Mail Innovation Lab suggests that stories have a longer persistence, with the essence of the story being recalled up to 20 days later.

The culture in many large organisations encourages 'sterilisation' of the messages we communicate to one another, and PowerPoint is probably the biggest culprit in this process. We are at pains to portray ourselves as rational beings, and have adapted the way we communicate accordingly. This is most pronounced in our formal professional communications, where we ensure that statements hang together in a rational sense while deliberately stripping out personal perspectives, value judgements and storylines.

In most organisations, storytelling happens but has gone underground. It is used mainly in informal situations where people feel more comfortable, while we revert to relatively formal language in the more formal situations of the office and work.

In some organisations, the power of the story has been recognised and they are seeing the story as a form of corporate nervous system that works in two directions – up and down – strengthening corporate identity and culture. Whereas formal communications convey instructions and 'content', the use of the story conveys morals and values: in other words, not just what should be done but why things should be done.

Stories are potent carriers of values and memory, and similar stories sometimes show up in more than one company. For instance, many companies share the story of the day an underling stops the boss from breaking a rule. In the Royal Mail version, Allan Leighton praises the local manager who forces him to go back to his car for identification. However, when a Revlon receptionist will not let Charles Revlon walk off with a sign-in sheet, he fires her. In one company the moral is, we obey rules; in the other, we obey rulers.

Is seems to be an accepted fact that few talents are more important to leadership and managerial success than knowing how to tell a good story.

As discussed in a number of chapters the importance and impact of storytelling has not been fully understood or exploited in a business context. The culture of an organisation is typically defined by the stories that are told – what people can and can't do, what is acceptable and what will happen if the written and unwritten rules are transgressed. Many organisations have a set of rules, and in some of the larger national government-owned companies these can take up whole libraries, although the advent of the Internet and intranet has meant that they have become more accessible. Even though all this information is available, the continuation of the company culture – the DNA of the company – is still passed from mouth to mouth.

So how can companies take advantage of these stories? Can they be used to the advantage of the company without the stigma of being 'spin'? My own belief is that they can, and I will discuss some of the tools and techniques I have developed to use the power of storytelling, in both a workshop situation and a more general situation.

So, what is a story?

A story is how human beings relate to each other on a day-to-day basis and relay information that is relevant and important to their survival, although I am not sure that the latter is wholly true in this day and age. In fact, there is probably no civilisation that doesn't use stories to preserve a common history, exchange knowledge, express a shared ethos and establish linguistic forms.

Stories have a structure that can be defined as follows:

- *A beginning*: this is the scene-setting, introducing the characters and establishing the expectation.
- *A middle*: in this section the 'meat' of the story should be told, and also the build-up to the last section.
- *The last bit*: this section covers the ending, the moral, and the 'sting' in the tail.
- *The conclusion*: this reiterates the story in a concise and understandable way.

There is also a structure to the elements that are required within the story:

- Stories should be told from an individual's perspective. Where stories are told from many perspectives they are less effective than those told from a single one. This goes back to the point discussed earlier about people empathising with the characters – seeing themselves in the situations.
- The story should challenge the listeners' preconceptions, providing a degree of strangeness or incongruity. It should arouse people's curiosity.
- The story must not only be strange, but also eerily familiar. If the story is too exotic, it will fail to engage the listener's attention and or to provide insight into his or her own situation.
- The story should, where possible, be true or at least credible. Where the story appears to be true, it has greater credibility and is therefore worth listening to.
- The story should be told as simply and as briefly as possible. The shorter the better, as many people have a short attention span

So how can stories be used effectively?

Using stories in workshops

Icebreaker

The children's game 'consequences' is the model here. Each participant adds to the story and in the process they all introduce themselves and their interests to the others. The facilitator or the first speaker sets the scene – where and when the story takes place – and then each of the other participants comes in as a character in the story, maybe providing some insight into his or her character. Lively and enduring stories and high energy emerge. The benefit of the icebreaker session is for the group to get to know each other and also to help the facilitator/advocate understand the dynamics of the group.

Feedback

To liven up what can be a very dull feedback session, ask teams to give feedback as a story, a fairy tale or a role-play. Many groups will initially find this quite difficult, but if you give them the frameworks to work from most will quickly latch on to the concept and produce excellent results. Not only will the feedback be entertaining but also the output will have persistence over time.

When running workshops for a major company, I decided one day to inject some humour into a fairly staid strategy development session. The session was very 'dry' and the fun factor was definitely not in evidence. The group had gone off in small teams to try and define what the vision for the particular strategy was going to be, and they were due to feed back some 45 minutes later. I announced that I wanted the feedback to be in the form of a short story or fairy tale. The look on the participants' faces was a picture to say the least, and protests were registered. But I asked them to persevere, try it to humour me.

One of the immediate effects was the level of noise from the teams – mainly laughter! They took up the challenge and dutifully 45 minutes later the feedback took place – what a difference from the traditional PowerPoint pitch. There was passion there and people were really engaged with what was happening. The vision was clear and concise, and of course as it was supposed to be a fairy tale there was a moral to the story at the end. The buzz around the group was noticeably different; there was much more laughing and joking and the presenting team continued to add to the storyline. I took the opportunity of following up with the whole group several times over the coming months and what was surprising was that the story stuck with them – even the moral at the end was still resonant.

The next time I used the technique, with a different group, I introduced an additional element – fancy dress outfits! The group wasn't instructed to use them; I just left them lying around and the group picked up on them and wove the characters into the story, adding yet another element. On other occasions I have introduced puppets, painting materials and Lego building blocks.

Rich pictures

Another feedback mechanism is to the use of a rich picture – a tableau or montage with pictures taken from magazines or the Internet. The picture should build a representation of the problem itself or the solution. Feedback using this media is typically a straight explanation/description of the image and how it was derived. See if you can get teams to create a story around the image.

As an extension to this technique I developed something I called 'media storming', which is similar to brainstorming but uses images instead of words (this is covered in more detail later in this section). To make this happen, I gather a whole range of magazines and other publications for the team to trawl for suitable images. The group then uses the images to produce a montage/collage of images which describe the problem or solution, whichever is the more appropriate. The group then describe to the rest of the group the collage/montage to explain their problem/solution.

Scenario

Get teams to build a story about the future that looks at the problem in hand. If the session is around building a strategy, create a story around what life or the company would be like if the strategy was successful. Alternatively, use a template to help structure thoughts. This could be a newspaper headline, a radar screen or a timeline – all are valid and will benefit from the addition of a story to bring out the salient points.

Scenarios are typically produced in groups of three or four that describe diametrically opposed views of the problem or solution. A matrix I have used a number of times with groups within large companies is shown in the figure below. This matrix looks at a mix of scenarios where the market is either growing or declining, and the company either introduces a new product or service or continues to produce only the existing product or service. Typically, using this matrix, four short stories would be produced of what could/would happen in 5–10 years if these strategic conditions prevailed.

There are many different forms of scenario, ranging from highly detailed and complex views of global economies developed and used by companies such as Shell, through to simple technology substitution/adoption scenarios used by communication companies. The level of complexity depends on the level of involvement within the organisation. Shell, at the peak of its scenario development, had over 100 people around the world involved in producing and maintaining scenario models.

Legends

By legends I mean stories told about the past from a future perspective which usually have a strong moral element. The legends tell how problems and issues were overcome, how foes were vanquished and

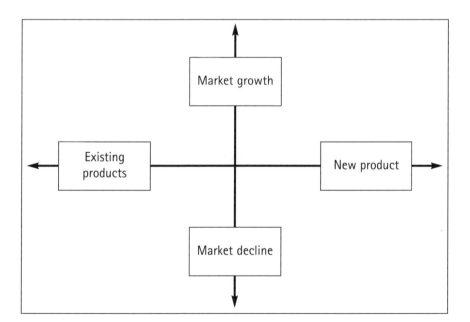

Figure 12 Scenario matrix

how heroes saved the day – all from a position sometime in the future.

The starting point for a legend exercise is the 'perfect' future state: the project was the most successful ever seen, the product or service storms the market or an individual or team takes all the honours.

A team will start by defining the end state: what is the perfect outcome of whatever it is that they are involved in. Then they start to look at the things that would be needed to bring that end state to a reality, and finally establish who the characters will be, who are the heroes of the piece and what they do. Once all this information is gathered a 'timeline' can be drawn, working backwards from the end.

The template only looks for four achievements and four characters that were involved, but this can be expanded to match different situations. However it is important to keep it simple and understandable, as the more complex it is the more difficult it will be to understand for those not involved in creating it. If the achievements are linked to a particular character and activity, then link them with lines on the template.

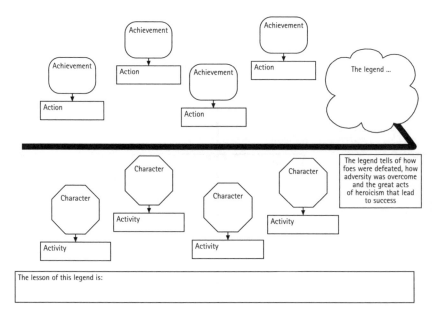

Figure 13 Legends

On the bottom of the template there is space for a moral or lesson that has been learned from the adventure. Again keep this simple and understandable.

Once the template has been completed the fun begins – putting the story itself together. There are a number of ways this can be achieved either individually or as a group. If it is done individually, someone just takes the template, sits down in a 'creative' space and develops the story. Sometimes it is easier if a model is taken from a film, book, children's story or the like, as this provides some of the key elements already formed.

In a group situation there are again several possible approaches. The first and probably the simplest is to form smaller groups of two or three people and get them to develop the story in a similar way to an individual. A more interesting way is to use what I term 'active story building', which is a little like a party game called 'consequences' in the UK. The group sit in a circle and the first person starts the story with a location, the second a time or time period, the third the main character and so on; each person adds an element to the story. To support this type of group working, I have used 'artists' to record the story as a wall painting, but it could just as easily be recorded using audio or video.

The use of props and 'vehicles'

One technique which I have seen used, and have used myself on many occasions to help in the story telling process – particularly when working with small groups (six to eight people) – is the use of some form of prop or set of props. These can range from fancy dress outfits to pictures and toys. I never force people to use these items, but I usually make them available to the group should they want to use them. Ninety per cent of the time they do and find them extremely useful.

So how would these be used? Many people find it difficult to tell a story. It is very often something that we haven't been trained to do, or if we have learned how to do it we have forgotten, as it was in our childhood. The use of the prop seems to allow people to tell the story through an inanimate object – somehow distancing the story-teller from what is being said. I have witnessed many examples of this being highly effective, and there are companies that specialise in this area. One such company is Lego, which not only manufactures children's building blocks but has set up something called 'Serious Play' (www seriousplay.com). This takes a highly structured approach to using the building blocks to get people to build stories – using the structures they build as metaphors for the problem, solution or situation.

Having experienced a couple of sessions with the Serious Play team I recognised the power of the method. However being a true Innovator I went away and invented my own, and of course, better way of using it!

Another medium I have seen used is art. Get people to draw or paint pictures of the strategy, issue or situation, and then change them to reflect their solution. Another way is through acting, where people are coached into first acting out the current situation and then the new, improved situation. In all these areas there are many companies that are specialising in such approaches. In each of them they are using something to channel the discussion, and placing the participants at a distance from the situation by using 'something' as a funnel for their thoughts and feelings. Many of the techniques take us back to our childhood where we didn't have learned behaviours and rules to restrict our thoughts.

Using stories in business

The use of stories in more general business can have a significant impact on the company. Many of the general corporate communications are filtered and tailored to meet the current company 'message', and although these are stories in their own right there is something about them that induces a degree of cynicism with the target audience. So why are the kind of stories I'm discussing here different?

The stories I have found extremely powerful when working with teams are those that are told about tomorrow – about things that are going to happen rather than things that have happened. To many people who are asked to participate in 'making up' a future type activity, the idea seems pointless or even ridiculous. 'How can we under-

	Yesterday	Today	Tomorrow
Non-fiction	Case study	Meeting	Plan
Enhanced reality		News	Strategic storytelling
Fiction	Legends		Scenario

Figure 14 Stories in business

stand what our future will be?' 'What will be will be'. Yet for some time now the concept of visualisation has been used by athletes to create their success. I was watching the Olympic bobsleigh team this year on TV and was fascinated to see the driver of the sleigh visualising the course before the run. He not only ran through it in his head but rehearsed the physical movements that would be required at each corner and twist along the way.

The concept of strategic storytelling is similar, in that it focuses on future success and then encourages the group to go through in their minds what they need to do at each 'corner', and more importantly to visualise success: what it would feel like to have achieved whatever it was that they were trying to do. This can take much iteration, as it is not something that people generally tend to be comfortable with. Although we can talk about the future, it is much harder to 'live' it.

The first step in strategic storytelling is to create the end point, whether this is a project, a strategy or a solution to a particular problem. As the Cheshire Cat said in that quote from *Alice's Adventures in Wonderland* in Chapter 1, if you don't know where the destination is then it doesn't matter what you do. So this first step is about creating the destination.

As an example let's take a project to build a new office building – something small then! The first questions I would ask in this sort of session would be:

- What are people doing?
- How are they acting?
- Is it a 'social' space?
- Do people like working in the building?
- Are people proud of the building?
- Is the building attractive?
- What is the atmosphere like – is it a lively place or is it silent and contemplative?
- What are the local press saying about the building?
- What is the industry saying about the company?
- What are the shareholders/stakeholders saying about the company?
- How does the company view the building?
- How has the building changed the company?

Once you have the answers to some of these questions you can start thinking about writing the story. For this example I am going to use the 'other people's shoes' template/methodology and the stories could go along the lines of:

Joe, an employee of Acme Insurance

It is a Monday morning and I can't wait to get into the new office. What a difference this new building has made to the company; the share price has increased 10 per cent since the building was opened. This has nothing to do with the building itself, but the staff are so much happier and this is reflected in the contact they have with the customers. I read over the weekend in the newspaper that the building has won an award for design or something. You know it made me feel so proud to be part of this company. I took the paper to the pub on Sunday to show my mates. One of them is thinking about trying to get a job as it looks like a 'cool' place to work. I told him that it was but I doubt if he would get a job as the company has been inundated with people wanting to work for us in the last few weeks. I am not so sure about this FUN thing but we will see; I have certainly met loads of new people through the programme and a few of us are getting together tonight to rehearse our new number for the band we've formed. Who would have thought we may be superstars next year!

Sharon, a customer of Acme Insurance

I have just called my insurance company and it made such a difference to be answered by somebody who was smiling – you can always tell when somebody is happy! I'd seen the article in the Sunday newspaper a couple of weeks ago and it was preying on my mind. The company had apparently built a new building that had won an award, and I was a bit bothered that my insurance premium might have gone up.

My friend came round the other day and she was telling me about a friend of hers who actually worked for the company. She was really excited about the new building that they had moved into; there had been a few teething problems but they had all been fixed now. She said the atmosphere in the company had changed so much and it was now a joy to go to work in the morning. People seemed genuinely excited to go to work!

I was really impressed and you are not going to believe this but I phoned up my stockbroker and bought some shares in the company – it really did seem like a company that was going somewhere – only time will tell though.

George, the finance director of the company

Another day another dollar – the last few months have been 'interesting'. The change in the company has been amazing since we implemented the FUN (Finding your Unifying Network) methodology [a fictional initiative only] when we opened the new building. There is a real buzz about the company and everyone seems excited about where we are going. OK there was a cost involved as usual, but we kept consultancy fees to a minimum and concentrated on things that would encourage the change we wanted. And now – well, we have only been in the building a few months but already the figures are looking very positive and you know we *are* having FUN in our new home.

Mary, a shareholder of the company

I was reading the newspaper this morning and I must admit I was a bit worried as shares in the company seemed to be a little unsteady when they announced the opening of the new building; I think the press thought it was a waste of money. I have invested a lot of my pension in the company and I am worried that I am not going to be able to survive if I lose any money. I have a friend who works there and she was the one who persuaded me to invest; she is so excited about what is happening I felt I just had to be part of it. Who knows, if what she says is true then the shares may take off – and then that holiday to the Caribbean may be a possibility after all.

John, the CEO of the company

We desperately needed to move buildings, and the local council offered us good incentives in the shape of grants if we moved into their area. Our old office was in need of some significant maintenance and we had found asbestos in one of the service ducts, which was going to cost a fortune to sort out. It was a great opportunity to build something that was not only functional but also looked good – an opportunity of a lifetime as my partner said. The staff were not too happy about moving, as for many of them it meant more travel and although the facilities would be better we were further away from the shopping centre. Meeting up with the FUN company at a conference last month gave me the idea of using the methodology to get people talking and create a sense of excitement about the move – and it worked. The staff seem happier, the figures are up and rising and we are up for the design award – what a great project!

Each of these stories provides a different take on one situation. What typically happens when companies go through planning and strategy cycles is that they only look at the impact on the company – things that they directly control. Using this technique to get people to look at things from different perspectives helps identify the wider impact of any initiative or strategy.

I have used this technique to look at an already formulated strategy. I call this strategy 'stress testing' and use it to assess how robust the strategy is in the face of external influences. It is more usually used to help companies understand the options and thereby help formulate strategy and plans.

Appendix 4

Frameworks, templates and tools

The use of frameworks and templates has become an integral part of the sticky Innovation way of working. When I started out on this journey I thought that creativity and Innovation, like many other things, were about a blank sheet of paper. What I quickly realised is that the majority of people need a framework within which to work, either mentally or physically. Sticky Innovation itself is a mental framework and in this Appendix I will discuss the concept of physical templates and their use in the sticky Innovation process.

Over the years, working in the Innovation arena, I must have created hundreds of templates for groups – typically taking a particular problem or issue and quickly creating something that would help frame the group's thoughts or highlight a particular point or set of information. For the purposes of this book, however, I will concentrate on the ones that have persisted over time – the ones that I still use frequently when working with groups and teams in the Innovation space.

The templates are typically printed up to A2 size or above and either laminated for regular use or printed for one-off use; alternatively where 'whiteboard walls' are available, they can be drawn up on them.

Timelines

I have found this to be one of the most powerful templates to use when asking a group or even an individual to work in the future

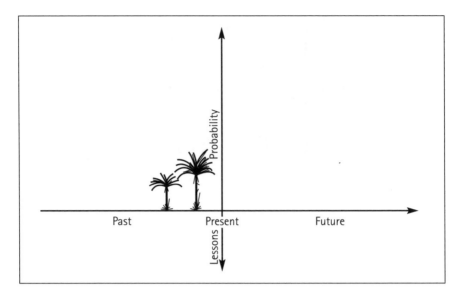

Figure 15 Timelines

space. There isn't anything very radical about this type of template, but it is a powerful way of sharing understanding and creating a shared vision. The horizontal axis is time: the past to the left and the future to the right. The vertical axis in the example shown shows probability above the line and lessons learned below the line. Time can be anything that is appropriate – typically from one to three years for project-type work and five to ten years for scenario-type activity.

The vertical axis above the line looks at the probability of events happening: the higher the item, the less the probability of it happening, and conversely the nearer the line, the higher the probability. I realise that this seems the wrong way round, but the less probable an idea is, the more it is in the clouds, and the stronger the possibility the more grounded it is. The area below the line I use for the lessons that have been learned or that are required.

For an example of how this template is used with a group, let's take the concept of a major project planning session. The template would first be used to look back at the history of the project – the things that have happened to get us to where we are today. They could be decisions that were taken, particular situations that had arisen, an individual who arrived, left or was promoted, and other such events or activities. The group would than be asked to write what lessons they had learned from these events below the line. Suppose, for example, that somebody joined and suddenly the project took off. The lesson from this event could be that this person, or this type of person, should have been brought in earlier.

People are usually comfortable with this phase of the activity, as it is just writing down what they already know and letting them get their particular view across. Just capturing this information is a powerful tool as it gets people to create this shared understanding. We each have information but we rarely get to write it down together, and the template provides a simple but effective framework to allow this to happen.

The template can also be used in other ways. One might be to get the group to look at the events they are aware of over the next five to ten years that may affect the particular project or initiative. These could be new technologies, market changes, competitor or government activities, events such as the Olympics or elections, or anything else that may influence how the project goes forward. Again, we use the vertical axis to delineate the probability the group are placing on the event: high probability events close to the base of the area and lower probability events higher – in the clouds!

In this case, the key events that would need to take place for the project to be successful would be recorded below the line. The group can then walk away with one chart that records the history and lessons, an analysis of the things that are going to influence/impact the project and the steps that need to be taken to make the vision a reality.

As I hope you can see, the template becomes a framework for bringing together a number of elements and it helps the group or individuals frame their thoughts, creating a shared vision and a shared understanding. When this template was first put together I had no idea what a powerful tool was being created. The framework allows people to structure their thoughts in such a way that they can draw insight from what has happened in the past and gain an understanding of what the 'real' things are that need to be done in the future.

Future radar

This template is an extension of the timeline and is particularly good when working with groups on scenarios, especially if the group has a natural tactical focus. The concept is that an individual, team or company is looking out over the next period of time – typically five to ten years – and there will be things on the horizon that are coming towards them. They are entered on the template with markers whose distance, size and colour are used to define how important they are. In the example shown I have used technology, society, resources and markets. However I have also found this very useful when combined with a PESTLE (political, economic, social, technological, legislative, environmental) analysis as it allows people to frame their thoughts and to look at how future events and actions may affect them as individuals.

To illustrate the use of the template I will walk through an example of somebody completing it from a personal perspective. There are many factors that could be considered, and a first step could be to use post-it notes to write down all the things that should be taken into account over the next five years. In this example the list may be long and may include such things as the Olympics in 2012, political elections, the introduction of high-definition TV, an insurance policy

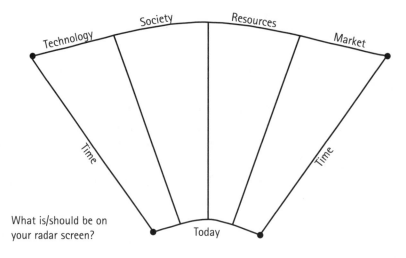

Figure 16 Personal radar

paying out, children finishing university, retirement and paying off of the mortgage among many others. Some of these events will be more important than others and typically they would be made to stand out. One approach is to use circles on the template with the size of the circle denoting the importance of the event and the colour denoting the potential impact.

This chart is particularly useful for explaining the future 'landscape' to senior managers as it gives them a quickly absorbed view of what may happen and what things they should be looking out for. I have found this really useful when trying to de-mystify technology as it gives people a framework to work with when reading newspaper, magazines or surfing the web. Although there is much information out there on what is happening in all areas, many people find it difficult to see the wood from the trees – what is important, what is useful and what is irrelevant.

Other people's shoes

This template was developed to try and get people or groups to look at an issue, strategy or activity through somebody else's eyes. The majority of people assume that everybody is like them: that they see the world in the same way, have the same values, associations and beliefs. This can lead to restrictive thinking and has in the past led to some amazingly bad decisions and marketing blunders – the fact that we think something is a good idea does not mean that everybody else does. This template does nothing more than prompt thinking and forces people to consider a proposition from different angles: in the example shown, the perspectives of the employer, the employee, the customer and the shareholder. When using the template the participants are asked to consider whatever it is they are working on from four viewpoints – how would these four groupings view the decision, strategy or issue. This can be done in a structured or unstructured way and other templates such as the radar template could be used in conjunction to further structure the thinking.

When using this template, feedback can be given in many ways but is particularly powerful when done either as a free-form story or as a rich picture, which is then used as a vehicle to structure the story.

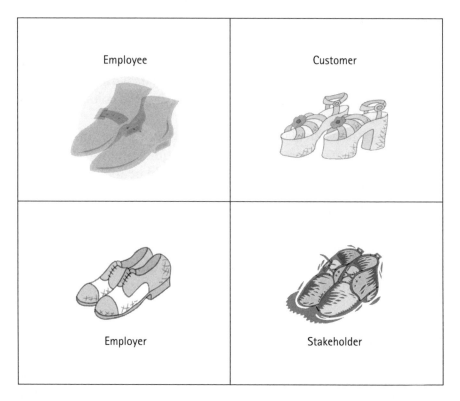

Figure 17 Other people's shoes

This technique can also be combined with others in this section – a timeline for each viewpoint and/or a legend could be used. They could also be considered individually or woven into something that brings all viewpoints together – typically a story or a timeline.

The strength of this approach is that it forces people to move outside their comfort zone and challenges their beliefs and values by getting them to see the world through somebody else's eyes.

War-gaming

This is focussed on getting teams to think differently – in fact so differently that they become their own competition. In this activity a team is told the company has fired them and that their task now is to drive it out of the market by setting up in competition. They should exploit the weaknesses of the old company and also take advantage of market conditions that may or will prevail.

The team then goes away and produce their business plan, using a traditional business plan framework. The plan should contain their vision and mission, the strategy, a market and sales strategy detailing the customer and/or customer groups that the new company will target, an employee strategy including a recruitment strategy, and lastly a communication and influencing plan. A deadline of 60 minutes is given for this work to be completed and a presentation is to be prepared for presentation to a venture capitalist who has been invited to hear it (usually role-played by a fellow facilitator). The group will inevitably challenge the timescale, but this cannot be altered as the venture capitalist 'has to get to another meeting'. The objective of the presentation is to gain funding for the new company.

Clearly the time constraint on this is a false one and you could choose to give people as much time as they wanted. However, I would guard against giving people too much time as they will delve into too much detail and undertake too much analysis, letting the left brain come to the fore rather than the more creative and inventive right brain.

Using this methodology it is amazing what the teams come up with. They build superb strategies that would certainly be effective in taking significant market share if they were brought into play. So why aren't these strategies developed for the parent company? What is it that stops these intelligent, articulate and rational people from persuading the company that it should do things differently? When that question is asked, a typical response is: 'It's not my job.' We are back again to self-limiting beliefs and the subject of permission.

Media storming

Media storming is an extension of brainstorming, but as the name suggests uses different forms of media – photos, printed text, video and audio. The idea came out of some work I was doing with team-building scenarios. I was looking for new ways to help the teams express their ideas other than the traditional reports or PowerPoint presentations.

Armed with a plentiful supply of magazines, I decided to get people to create montages and rich pictures of their alternative futures. As we were doing this, one of the teams took an article in the magazine and decided to use it as a catalyst to talk about how their particular solution could solve whatever the problem was in the article. They reported back to the rest of the group who picked up this idea of using articles and images to help stimulate ideas about their solutions too. By the end of the workshop we had seemingly solved Third World hunger!

The way the technique works is to pick a media article, news website or movie scene at random, and look at how your solution, situation or idea could help or hinder the topic of the medium. Using movie scenes can expand the technique, as can children's storybooks and whatever other media are available. This is particularly powerful when feeding back as it can show that the work is 'grounded' in some form of reality – especially as it helps people understand whatever it is that you want to tell them about.

The technique has developed into using other media and particularly the Internet, and has proved useful in prompting real left-field thinking – getting radical thoughts into areas where 'group-think' has developed.

Action planning

As stated many times in this book, the impact of any Innovation or Innovative activities is dependent on the actions that take place after the concept has been developed. Traditional action-planning techniques are valid, but to really make the Innovation stick the action-planning phase of any initiative needs to be sticky too. So what sort of action plan will ensure maximum benefit is obtained from the concept or activity?

Traditional action plans tend to be formal, long, detailed and generally ignored. The mere sight of a detailed action plan has, for many, an adverse effect, usually resulting in their eyes glazing over as they think of something, anything more interesting. Although this is a very sweeping statement I have seen this effect so many times in meetings: one or two people are very engaged and the rest of the room lean back away from the table – the body language says 'I really don't want to be part of this'.

Although the detailed action plan is highly relevant for those at the sharp end of any initiative, the obsession that typically occurs means that the all-important end state, the vision, is lost. The initiative loses strategic drive and becomes a task-driven activity. In fact on many occasions the tasks become the initiative rather than the other way round!

An example is what happened at a major UK corporation that I was involved in. The company decided that they needed a single customer database – a single view of the customer. An audit within the company eventually, after much analysis and searching, found that customer information was stored in well over 3000 places. This resulted in confusion when trying to manage the customer relationship. It actually placed customers in a strong position as they realised that they could play one part of the company off against the other – it was estimated that the company had 'given away' several million pounds in discounts against itself!

A team of six people were pulled together with a main Board member heading up the initiative. Of course a team of consultants who had implemented such systems before was engaged to 'help' guide the project through to a successful end state. The small team, assisted by the consultants, built a vision of what should be achieved and wrote a very compelling business case for an investment in the resources – people, technology, training etc. – that would be required.

The investment was somewhere in the region of £250,000 and the project would pay back in less than two years in terms of improved customer relationships, higher sales and increased efficiency. Within six weeks the project had grown to 150 people, the customer requirements phase had extended from one month to 10, and the budgetary requirements had tripled.

What had happened? What had become of the simple vision that had been created? Well, it had been turned into a project and had built a life of its own. The project ran for more than four years. It never delivered its goals; its costs spiralled to over £4m and it ended with over 350 people involved on the project. The technology that was specified in the original remit had been superseded several times and the Internet and the World Wide Web had become a de facto interface standard, all in the time the project was due to deliver.

Were the people involved in the project at fault? Was the contract wrong? Was it the suppliers' fault? Of course there was much soul searching, but no one was sacked for it because committees had taken all the decisions and it was difficult to point the finger at any one person or role. So how did it go so awry? The people had just lost the vision; they had got bogged down in the detail, thriving on the day-to-day minutiae of the project. They had forgotten what it was they were actually trying to create – a customer database. All the meetings were about terminals and fields, bits and offsets, spend and penalties, and nothing about the customer at all.

How could the action plan have been different?

It is vital that the action plan is focussed on the desired outcome of the project or initiative rather than the detail of the 'how'. Of course there is a place for detailed plans but these should be subordinated to the overall action plan. I have worked with true masters of this who would start and close every project meeting with a review of where they are against the overall vision for the project. This is what was communicated up to the director or whoever was responsible, not the detail that I have seen main board directors have to sit through – endless Gannt charts, Excel spreadsheets and project reports that would take half a tree to produce – Ok, slight exaggeration!

The secret of a good action plan is to have no more than six to eight points on it, supported by whatever detail is thought to be of interest to the recipient in a separate document or documents. Don't include everything 'just in case'; that just overwhelms people (which is a strategy in itself that I have seen used – if I send him so much he can't be bothered to read it then my back is covered if anything goes wrong!). At the top of the action plan should be the overall goal or vision statement: whatever the project or initiative is trying to achieve. At the bottom of the plan is a short one-line statement that gives a view of where the project is at.

Only highlight the things that will affect the overall goal of the project, not the detail about the colour of the widgets which, although they may be important to the project team, have no interest for the sponsor.

I once worked for a manager who gave me one of the most valuable pieces of advice I have ever had in my business career. Any report should be no more than four to six sides of A4 paper with a summary on the first sheet. Why choose these numbers? Well his view was that no one ever reads past page four of any document. Whether this is true or not I don't know, but it has stood me well in my career so far.

So to recap. Action plans should be relevant and to the point. They should contain the vision and or goal of the project or initiative. They should contain no more than six or eight points. The points should be clearly articulated as to how they affect the goal and their status should be made clear – are they on target or off. There should be a summary at the bottom of the sheet that gives the project manager/ director's view of the project and how it is progressing against the vision/goal.

Appendix 5

Creativity tools and techniques

I have covered many creativity tools and techniques already in the book but I will bring them together in this section for reference. As previously mentioned I have distilled the many hundreds of tools and techniques down to five main groupings which, if used correctly, will provide all you should need to stimulate creative thinking. There are many, many more and if this is something you are particularly interested in a search on Google will provide more than enough material for anyone.

My five groups of creativity techniques are:

- *Parallels*: looking for parallels with other topics/areas.
- *Inversion/reversals*: turning the problem or parts of the problem upside down.
- *Randomness*: introducing random stimulation through pictures, words etc.
- *Disassembly*: looking at the component parts of the problem and analysing them.
- *Constraints*: introducing false constraints – half the cost, half the size, twice as fast and so on.

Each of these groupings masks the complexity that can exist behind it, and I would guess that people will be finding new ways to stimulate creative thinking on a daily basis – I know I do from time to time. However let's stick to the five main groups and look at how they might be applied to a problem.

The problem I am going to work though is that of litter in town centres, a problem that is relevant anywhere in the world – well almost anywhere. So which creativity techniques and tools could you use and how would you use them? Well the answer is all of them and it depends, in that order!

The first thing to do is define what the problem is.

- Using the *parallels* technique you could look at how other towns have solved the problem. Maybe not in your country – maybe in sub-Saharan Africa even. You could also look at what other things people drop.
- Using the *inversions/reversals* technique you may look at how to get people to pick litter up, how you could make litter valuable. Another angle is how could you get people to drop litter elsewhere and not in the town, maybe at home.
- Using the *randomness* technique it may be that you introduce a random picture or object – maybe a picture of a clown, which would prompt some ideas around making the litter entertaining, giving theatre vouchers for people who don't drop litter or who pick it up. Run a competition to turn the litter into art to be exhibited at the Tate Gallery in London.
- When using the *disassembly* technique you may start to look at what litter is and who drops it. Is it certain people or groups of people? Where do they drop it – is it only in specific locations or is it everywhere?
- The *constraints* technique might look at how to have no packaging, or no people in towns and so on.

One method I have found for recording the output from these types of creativity sessions is to create a simple mind map chart to group the ideas around topic areas.

As you can see, these creativity tools and techniques can turn a simple problem into a whole raft of alternative questions. Any one of these topics could generate different solutions and analyses of the 'landscape'.

Is it that people are dropping litter, that there are no receptacles for people to put litter in, that people don't care about their environment, that dropping litter is 'cool', that people think that it is decorative and makes the place look better, that there is nobody to clear the litter? The list could go on and on. As you can see, any one of these questions could generate a whole different set of solutions, and it may be that you have to go through a few cycles and ask many questions before you find the answer.

Note

1. Myers-Briggs is a framework for understanding individuals' preferences in a range of situations. People are placed in one of 16 boxes depending on a detailed assessment that seeks to draw out the ways people like to behave and think. Further details can be found at www.myers-briggs.com, and there are many qualified assessors who can be accessed through this site. A further way of accessing this framework is to complete the questions online at www.human metrics.com which is a site that provides the service for free, although the assessment given on the site should be used with care.

References

Davila, Tony, Epstein, Marc J. and Shelton, Robert (2006) *Making Innovation Work: How to Manage It, Measure It, and Profit from It.* Upper Saddle River: Wharton School Publishing.

Hoff, B. (1982) *The Tao of Pooh.* New York: Dutton Books.

Pease, A. and Pease, B. (2001) *Why Men Don't Listen and Women Don't Read Maps.* New York: Broadway Books.

Schumpeter, J. (1934) *The Theory of Economic Development.* Cambridge, Mass.: Harvard University Press.

Surowiecki, J. (2004) *The Wisdom of Crowds.* New York: Random House.

Index